To Conquer is To Live

To Conquer is To Live

The Life of Captain John Smith of Jamestown

KIERAN DOHERTY

Twenty-First Century Books
Brookfield, Connecticut

To my wife, Lynne, for her steadfast, loving, and joyous support not only during the writing of this book but in all my life. And to my editor, Amy Shields, whose steady understanding makes an often lonely process much less lonely.

Cover photographs courtesy of North Wind Picture Archives and New York Public Library Picture Collection

Photographs courtesy of Guildhall Library, Corporation of London, UK/Bridgeman Art Library, Panorama of London and the Thames, c. 1600 engravings by Nicholas Visscher (Claes) Jansz, 1586-1652): pp. 10 (part two showing St. Paul's Cathedral and the Globe Theatre), 11 (part three showing Southwark, London Bridge and the churches in the City); Hulton Getty/Liaison Agency: p. 18; New York Public Library Picture Collection: pp. 23, 100; Corbis-Bettman: pp. 25, 66, 92, 122; The Mariners' Museum, Newport News, VA: p. 31; © Sidney King: pp. 37, 48; The Granger Collection, New York: pp. 52, 75, 82, 85, 106, 109, 117; National Park Service, Colonial National Historical Park: p. 58; National Portrait Gallery, Smithsonian Institution/Art Resource, NY: p. 119; North Wind Picture Archives: p. 125

Library of Congress Cataloging-in-Publication Data
Doherty, Kieran.
To conquer is to live : the life of Captain John Smith of Jamestown / Kieran Doherty.
p. cm.
Includes bibliographical references and index.
ISBN 0-7613-1820-8 (lib. bdg.)
1. Smith, John, 1580–1631—Juvenile literature. 2. Colonists—Virginia—Jamestown—Biography—Juvenile literature. 3. Jamestown (Va.)—History—17th century—Juvenile literature. 4. Jamestown (Va.)—Biography—Juvenile literature. 5. Virginia—History—Colonial period, ca. 1600–1775—Juvenile literature. 6. Explorers—America—Biography—Juvenile literature. 7. Explorers—England—Biography—Juvenile literature. [1. Smith, John, 1580–1631. 2. Explorers. 3. Jamestown (Va.)—History. 4. Virginia—History—Colonial period, ca. 1600–1775.] I. Title.
F229.S7 D64 2001 973.2'1'092—dc21 00-044309

Published by Twenty-First Century Books
A Division of The Millbrook Press, Inc.
2 Old New Milford Road
Brookfield, Connecticut 06804
www.millbrookpress.com

Copyright © 2001 by Kieran Doherty
All rights reserved
Printed in the United States of America
1 3 5 6 4 2

✦ Contents ✦

❖ Introduction ❖

No figure in American history has suffered more at the hands of the mythmakers than Captain John Smith.

Ask virtually any American what he or she knows about John Smith, and the first response you will get is a retelling of the story of how Pocahontas threw herself on top of Smith to keep her father's Indian braves from killing the English settler. Unfortunately, this story—elevated to the level of myth in the almost four centuries since Smith walked the landscape of the Virginia Tidewater region—is as far as most people's knowledge of Smith goes.

That is a shame, for there is much, much more to the story of Captain John Smith than this admittedly remarkable incident. Indeed, Smith lived a full and exciting life both before and after his time in Virginia. His would have been a remarkable life, a life worthy of note, even without the Pocahontas story as its centerpiece.

Until just a few years ago, I knew no more about Smith than most other Americans. Then I had occasion to read about John Smith's life and travels and adventures. As I read, I became convinced that Smith had been shortchanged by history. And I became convinced that I wanted to tell Smith's true story.

In telling this story, I have quoted extensively from John Smith's own writings, collected in a two-volume anthology popularly known as *John Smith's Works*, edited by Edward Arber.

In adding substance and humanity to my portrait of Smith, I relied heavily on two biographies. *The Three Worlds of Captain John Smith*, by Philip Barbour, is a scholarly work I found particularly helpful in writing about Smith's life and adventures before he came to Virginia. *Captain John Smith*, by Bradford Smith, provided me with much valuable information about John Smith's surroundings in England.

Always a man of action, John Smith wrote extensively about his adventures, but he wrote very little about his feelings. As a consequence, I was forced, throughout this book, to speculate about Smith's interior life. These speculations and surmises were made using my own common sense, backed up by research into Smith and his times. In every instance, these speculations are clearly indicated in the text.

In quoting, I changed Smith's original language as little as possible, in an attempt to re-create the "music" of the English language as spoken by John Smith and his contemporaries. Readers should remember that writers in Smith's time spelled phonetically. If a word "looks" strange, simply sound it out as you read.

A note about dates: Smith and his contemporaries used what is today known as the Old Style calendar. According to this calendar, the New Year started on March 25, not January 1. That means that what John Smith would have called January 1600 would actually have been January of 1601. At the same time, this Old Style calendar reckoned dates of days of the month differently. The date Smith knew as June 15 would actually have been June 25, according to our calendar.

In this book the days of the month are given according to the Old Style calendar, while years are given according to the New Style calendar.

CHAPTER ONE

Beginnings

John Smith was born in 1580 in the tiny farming village of Willoughby in the county of Lincolnshire on England's east coast. Like much of John Smith's story, the exact date of his birth is lost in the distant past. We do know, however, that he was christened in the local parish church on January 9 of that year, so it is safe to assume he was born early that same month.

John was the first-born child of an English farmer named George Smith and his wife, Alice. While far from wealthy, the Smith family, which soon included a second son and a daughter, were better off than most English farmers near the end of the sixteenth century. They lived in a large home furnished with candlesticks of pewter and brass, several wooden chests, four chairs, an extra table, and a cupboard. At a time when many rural families still slept on straw, they had feather beds and plenty of linens. Curtains covered their windows, and paintings—called "painted cloaths"—decorated their walls.

George Smith, John's father, seems to have enjoyed a close relationship with Peregrine Bertie, Lord Willoughby, the lord of the manor of Willoughby. Though the Smiths were far below the Berties in social standing, and though it was almost unheard of in sixteenth-century England for the classes to mix, indications are that Lord Willoughby and George Smith were

London in the Elizabethan Age: St. Paul's Cathedral, the Globe Theatre, and

friends as well as landlord and tenant. Such a relationship could only have helped George Smith and his family financially, and would prove to help John Smith as he grew to manhood.

At the age of about six, Jack, as he was undoubtedly called, started school, enrolling in a so-called ABC school where he learned to read and write and do simple sums. A few years later, he enrolled in a Latin, or grammar, school not far from his family's farm.

School in John Smith's time was very different from school today. Students were in class from about seven o'clock in the morning until about five in the afternoon, with just one short

London Bridge stand watch over a city busy with trade, culture, and exploration.

recess in mid-morning and a half hour or so for lunch. Lessons were taught by repetition. Students who misbehaved or whose work did not please the schoolmaster were caned.

School must have been torture for young John. He was—by his own admission—a dreamer who longed for a life of travel, a life filled with adventures and excitement. John Smith's dreams were not just a way to take his mind off his schoolwork. His dreams became an overwhelming desire for a life of action and romance. They were to guide his entire life, and making those dreams come true was to lead him not only to adventure, but also to a place in history.

It's not surprising that John dreamed of a life filled with adventure. He was born in what we call the Elizabethan Age, a time when Englishmen could dream as they had never dreamed before. Queen Elizabeth I, the daughter of King Henry VIII, had been on the throne for more than two decades. Under her rule, England was becoming one of Europe's great powers. Seamen like Sir Francis Drake and Thomas Cavendish—the first two Englishmen to circumnavigate the globe—were finding fame and fortune on the world's oceans. Explorers like Sir Walter Raleigh were staking Elizabeth's claim to far-off lands. Little wonder, then, that John Smith looked to a life beyond his father's farm.

When he was about thirteen years old John decided to run away. "(H)is minde being even then set upon brave adventures, [he] sould his Satchell, bookes, and all he had, intending secretly to get to Sea. . . . ," Smith later said, writing in the third person, as many authors did in those days.[1] This attempt to run away was foiled by John's father, who learned of his plans, stopped him, and dragged him back to work on the family farm.

Though John undoubtedly kept dreaming of adventure, he was unable to leave home for good until 1596, when his father died. At the age of sixteen, he suddenly found himself with what he described as "libertie enough . . . to get beyond the Sea."[2]

There was little, apparently, to keep John at home. His actions prove he was not much interested in being a farmer like his father. At the same time, there seemed to be ill feelings between John and his mother. Perhaps he felt that Alice Smith betrayed the memory of his father when she remarried very soon after George Smith's death. To be sure, such a quick second (and even third and fourth) marriage was not unusual in those days, when both husbands and wives died young. John Smith, however, seems to have been so upset by his mother's remarriage that, as far as we know, he never spoke to his mother again. In fact, it seems likely from John Smith's later life that what he viewed as his mother's betrayal of his father may well have made him distrust women. Smith, as we shall see, never married, though he obviously liked women and they, just as obviously, were drawn to him.

During this period of John's life, the Protestant people of the Netherlands, just a hundred miles or so across the North Sea from Lincolnshire, were fighting a bloody war to gain their freedom from Roman Catholic Spain. Thousands of Protestant Englishmen volunteered to serve as soldiers on the side of the Dutch against the Spanish. Some time not long after his father's death, John Smith became one of those volunteers and boarded a ship bound for the Netherlands. His goal, he later wrote, was to learn what he called "the rudiments of warre."[3]

Once in the Netherlands, John joined a company of infantry under the command of an English mercenary officer. While Smith left no record of his experiences in battle we can assume from his later accomplishments as a fighting man that he learned a great deal.

In any event, by 1599 nineteen-year-old John was back in England, once again living in Willoughby. Not long after his return he learned that Lord Willoughby was seeking a paid companion to accompany his sons, Peregrine and Robert Bertie, on a tour of France. Still seeking adventure and, no doubt, remembering that his father, in his will, had charged him to "honoure and love my . . . good Lord Willoughbie during his lyfe . . . ," John offered his services.[4] His offer was accepted and soon John Smith found himself once again bound for the European continent.

The trip to Europe seems not to have gone very well. Perhaps John was uncomfortable around the wealthy Bertie brothers. Or perhaps he resented taking orders from them. Whatever the cause, after about six weeks the Bertie brothers gave him enough money to pay for his return journey and sent him home.

In Europe with a few coins in his purse and a chance for adventure at hand, John was in no rush to return to England.

Instead, he went to Paris. After a few weeks in the French capital he made his way to Holland and then departed for Scotland, where he hoped to gain a position as a courtier in the court of King James VI.

As was to be the case again and again in John Smith's life, his plans soon went awry. As the ship neared the Scottish coast, it was struck by one of the fearsome storms that regularly sweep across the North Sea. The wind and waves drove the ship onto the wild, rocky coast of a tiny island just off the coast not far from the port city of Berwick.

John was either injured in the shipwreck or fell ill soon after his rough landing, for he spent several weeks recuperating—probably in the hut of a friendly fisherman—before making his way to the Scottish mainland. Once there, he attempted to gain entry to the Scottish court. No one, however, was willing to recommend the son of an English farmer as a courtier. John later wrote that with neither "money nor meanes to make him a Courtier; he returned to Willoughby in Lincoln-shire."[5]

John was a popular young man in his home village when he returned from his European travels. Other villagers seem to have besieged him with questions about his experiences fighting against the Catholic forces of Spain, about life in the Low Countries, and about Paris and the Parisians.

John soon grew tired of all the questions and socializing. "[W]ithin a short time being glutted with too much company, wherein he took small delight," he later wrote, "he retired himself into a little wooddie pasture."[6]

In that "wooddie pasture"—probably a field owned by Lord Willoughby—he set about the business of becoming a gentleman-knight like the famous knights of King Arthur's Round Table. He hired the services of a local man who served as his squire. He built, he tells us in his brief autobiography, a "Pavillion of boughes," and in this leafy shelter he lived a hermit's life, at least for a time.[7] For reading material, he had two books. The first of these was *The Art of War*, by the Italian statesman Nicolo Machiavelli. The second was a collection of inspirational sayings by the great Roman emperor-philosopher Marcus Aurelius.

John lived in that field for several months, studying and practicing the arts and crafts of knighthood. He had a horse and, he tells us, a lance he used to practice mounted combat.

Word of John's strange behavior in the woods must have made its way to Lord Willoughby. The lord, it seems, arranged for John to take lessons in horsemanship and mounted combat from Theodore Polaloga, an Italian riding master in the service of the Earl of Lincoln. John, in his autobiography, simply said that "friends" persuaded Polaloga to become his tutor. However, given the fact that Polaloga was one of the most famous horsemen in Europe, it seems very likely that only Lord Willoughby could have made arrangements for the lessons, given at Tattershall Castle, the house of the Earl of Lincoln, not far from Willoughby.

From Polaloga John learned to ride as if he and his horse were one creature, and to wield a sword and lance while his mount raced along at full speed. He learned to force his horse to turn on a shilling and to jump and rear at the touch of his heels.

From Polaloga John also learned of great battles then being fought between Christians and the Turks in Eastern Europe. As the riding master and his pupil sat together at the end of a day's practice, Polaloga's war stories would have stirred John's blood.

To be sure, John had no desire to fight again in a war between Protestants and Catholics. He was, he said, "both lamenting and repenting to have seene so many Christians slaughter one another" in the battles in the Netherlands. A war in which Christians fought Turks who were—at least to John's way of thinking—heathens, was a different matter. And so, in mid-1600, "desirous to see more of the world, and trie his fortune against the Turkes," John Smith decided to leave Willoughby again, this time for Hungary.[8]

Though John could not have known it when he decided to leave Willoughby in 1600, he was about to embark on a three-and-a-half-year adventure. In those years, John Smith, the farmer's son from Willoughby, would earn a measure of the fame and fortune he desired while he learned lessons he would later need to survive in the untamed wilderness of Virginia.

CHAPTER TWO

Soldier, Slave, Wanderer

When John Smith left England again in the summer of 1600, The Netherlands was his first stop on a journey that would eventually take him more than one thousand miles across Europe all the way to Russia.

Smith's adventures began almost as soon as he arrived in Holland. There, as he arranged passage on a ship bound for France, he met four young Frenchmen he described as "Gallants."[1] These well-dressed and well-mannered young men told Smith that they, too, were on their way to fight the Turks. They suggested that they all travel together to present themselves to the duchess of Mercoeur, wife of the commander of the Christian forces in Hungary. The duchess, they said, would surely give them letters of introduction to her husband.

In truth, the four men John described as gallants were thieves. Soon after the ship that carried them down the coast to France arrived in port, the four relieved Smith of all his belongings except for the clothes on his back. They also stole all his money except for a single penny.

For the next several weeks Smith was forced to beg for money and food as he trudged across France to the port city of

In some of his later writings, Smith describes with relish how he helped la Roche and his crew capture a Venetian vessel laden with a treasure in silk, gold, and silver coins. This picture shows a black-flagged pirate ship overtaking a trading vessel.

Marseilles. There he secured passage on a ship carrying Roman Catholic pilgrims to Italy.

If John Smith thought his troubles were over once he turned his back on France, he was sadly mistaken. No sooner had the ship left port than a terrible storm struck, forcing the vessel to anchor behind an island. Frightened, the ship's Catholic passengers decided that the storm was a sign that God was displeased with them for allowing Smith—a Protestant, and a hated Englishman, as well—on board the vessel. Without ceremony, they threw him overboard. Luckily, Smith was able to swim to the island and take refuge on its shores with, he said, "a few kine [cattle] and goats" that lived there.[2]

When the sun rose the next morning, Smith spied two other ships riding at anchor near the island. The captain of one of those vessels, a man named la Roche, took him on board. The vessel soon weighed anchor and made her way to Alexandria, in Egypt, where the vessel's cargo was unloaded.

Apparently Captain la Roche wanted more profits than he'd gained delivering cargo. Leaving Alexandria, with Smith still a member of the crew, la Roche turned pirate. Steering a course between Italy and Yugoslavia, he set out in search of vessels he could capture and loot. Smith, for his part, saw nothing wrong with this foray into piracy, so long as it was carried out against non-English ships.

Following this adventure, Smith was put ashore in Italy. As a reward for his part in the taking of a Venetian ship, he was paid the equivalent of £225 in gold, a small fortune at a time when an English yeoman farmer earned about £40 per year. His part of the booty also included a small box, probably of gold, worth an equal amount.

Well financed and, no doubt, sporting a fine new suit of clothes and a fancy sword, Smith traveled across Italy, made his way by ship to Yugoslavia, and then journeyed on foot to Hungary. There, about six months after his departure from England, he joined a Protestant regiment that was attempting to help the besieged town of Oberlimbach in the south of Hungary.

At Oberlimbach, Smith soon became acquainted with Baron Hans Jacob Kisell, the commander of the army that was trying to relieve the Christians in the city. Calling on knowledge he'd gained from his reading of military texts, Smith showed Kisell a way that torches could be used to signal the besieged Christians when an attack was about to begin. He also convinced the baron that he could give the Turks a distorted idea of the number of attacking Christians by burning several thousand of the fuses carried by soldiers in battle and used to light the matches of their matchlock muskets. The enemy, seeing the burning fuses, would believe they were facing a much larger force than they actually were.

Smith's ideas worked perfectly. Kisell signaled the forces inside the city informing them of his plan to attack the Turkish army. At a signal from the baron, some three thousand matches were set on fire. When the Turks saw the burning matches, Smith later wrote, they "ranne up and downe as men amazed."[3] As the Turks panicked, Kisell's army and the Christians inside the city mounted their joint attack. In minutes, the Turks were routed.

As a reward for his part in the battle, John Smith was promoted to the rank of captain and put in command of 250 horsemen. At the age of twenty, he had found at least some of the fame that had been his goal since he was a boy daydreaming in his grammar school classroom.

Soon after that battle, Smith joined an army trying to capture a walled city not far from what is now the border between Austria and Hungary. Once again, he made use of a strategy he'd learned in his reading. He created devices like modern artillery shells. These devices (he called them "fiery Dragons") were basically clay pots filled with gunpowder and musket balls and covered with cloth and pitch.[4] Set afire, they were lobbed over the city's walls using catapults.

"[I]t was a fearfull sight to see the short flaming course of their flight in the aire," Smith wrote, adding that after the fiery dragons landed in the town and exploded, "the lamentable noise of the miserable slaughtered Turkes was most wonderful to heare."[5] Indeed, the Turks soon surrendered the town to the Christian army.

From March to some time in June 1602, Smith found himself part of a large Christian force trying to capture a city in Hungary. For a month, he and the other Christian soldiers dug trenches and erected mounds of earth on which they could place cannon to attack the city. As they labored, Turkish warriors mocked them from the ramparts. Eventually, one of the Muslim leaders—a man identified by Smith as Lord Turbashaw—sent a challenge to the Christian army. "(T)he Lord Turbashaw," Smith later wrote, "did defie any Captaine, that had the command of a Company, who durst combat with him for his head."[6]

Today the idea of single-handed combat between champions seems strange. Yet in Smith's time, such combat was not unusual.

According to Smith, there was competition among the Christians to see who would meet Lord Turbashaw in battle. Eventually lots were drawn and he was the "winner."

The battle took place on the plain before the city. To the sound of horns, Smith later wrote, Turbashaw, "entered the field well mounted and armed" with a great pair of wings made of eagle feathers trimmed in silver fixed to his armor at the shoulders.[7] A servant walked before him carrying his lance while two others walked beside his horse. Smith came to the field of battle encased in armor, with only a page to carry his lance.

The fight itself was quick. When the champions charged, Smith said, he "passed the Turke throw the sight of his [helmet], face, head and all, that he fell dead to the ground."[8] In short order, Smith dismounted, ripped off Turbashaw's helmet and took his head as a trophy.

Enraged by the outcome of this duel, a warrior named Grualgo issued a challenge to Smith, saying he would either win back Turbashaw's head or lose his own. Smith had no choice but to accept this second challenge.

Again he was the victor, and again he took the Turk's head as his prize.

Smith, feeling cocky and sure of himself, then issued a challenge of his own, daring any warrior in the city to come forth and face him in man-to-man battle. A Turk with the unlikely name (as written by Smith) of Bonny Mulgro accepted the challenge. Following a terrible fight, Mulgro, too, lost his head.

With the three heads he'd taken as trophies mounted on lances, Smith was conducted to the tent of General Moses Szekely, the Christian commander. There he was awarded a horse and a valuable scimitar. Later, Prince Sigismund Bathory, the commander in chief of the Christian forces, rewarded him with a small fortune in gold and coin. Even more important, as far as John Smith was concerned, he was also awarded a coat of arms. With this coat of arms—decorated with three Turks heads in honor of his single-handed victories—John Smith, the son of a simple farmer, earned the right to call himself a gentleman.

It was probably at this time that John Smith created his personal motto to go along with his new coat of arms. That motto, *Vincere est Vivere*, means "to conquer is to live."

It has to be noted that for years some historians doubted Smith's account of this period. Recent research, however, has proved the truth of many of his claims. As remarkable as his tale is, then, there is no reason to doubt its truth.

These exploits in single-handed combat marked the high-point of Smith's career as a soldier in Hungary. In late 1602, shortly after he won his coat of arms, he was captured in battle and sold into slavery.

Purchased by a wealthy Turk from Constantinople, John Smith was made servant to his new master's mistress, a woman Smith identifies as Charatza Tragabigzanda. This woman (Smith would later name an island off the coast of New England in her honor) was a "Noble Gentlewoman" who treated her new slave kindly.[9] She conversed with him in Italian, a smattering of which he must have learned in his travels, and took care to see he was comfortable. This time as

This etching shows John Smith taken into slavery by Charatza's brother, who stripped him naked and shaved his head.

the young lady's slave, however, did not last long. Afraid that her mother would notice her kindness toward Smith and take vengeance on him, she sent him to serve her brother, a minor ruler in Turkey.

According to Smith, Charatza sent instructions to her brother that he should be treated kindly. Instead, Charatza's brother forced him to wear an iron ring riveted around his neck. With his long curly hair and full beard shaved off, he was made, Smith said, "Slave of slaves to them all."[10]

From his first day in Turkey, Smith must have dreamed of escape. An opportunity, however, did not present itself until the fall of 1603, when crops were being harvested. As Smith worked in the fields, Charatza's brother began beating him. Enraged, Smith fought back and killed his master with a threshing bat (a tool used to separate wheat from chaff).

Quickly, Smith stripped the dead Turk of his clothes and put them on. He hid the body beneath a pile of straw, filled a knapsack with grain he could use as food, and fled on horseback.

For the next two and a half weeks, Smith was a fugitive, traveling in constant fear of discovery. Somehow he avoided capture and made his way to Russia, where, he later wrote, he was befriended by a local governor who struck off his neck irons and, in Smith's words, "kindly used him."[11]

Some time in early 1604, armed with a certificate of safe passage from the governor, Smith headed for England. It would seem that by this time he would have had all the adventure he wanted and that he would have been happy to go straight home. Instead, he spent the next several weeks wandering through Russia, Lithuania, and Poland before making his way to Hungary, where he found his former commander, Prince Bathory. The prince, who must have thought Smith dead, rewarded him for his recent hardships by giving him the equivalent of about £500. He also gave Smith a written certificate proving that he had been awarded his coat of arms.

Leaving Hungary, John Smith continued sightseeing, visiting Germany, France, Spain, and North Africa. There, he took passage on a French ship of war. Even now, bound for home, Smith could not seem able to avoid adventures. When the French ship was forced into the open Atlantic by storms, her captain decided to attack Spanish shipping. In the waters near the Canary Islands, the French man-of-war engaged two Spanish warships in a fierce, two-day battle. Though the French vessel was boarded and set on fire, her crew—including Smith—repelled the boarders, put out the fires set by the Spanish, and slipped away, though twenty-seven of her crewmen were killed in the fighting.

*The four corners of this etching are adorned
with symbols of Smith's life: a group of colonists, a globe,
a ship, and a charging horse.*

The French vessel, badly battered by shot, somehow managed to limp into port at Safi, Morocco. There, in late 1604, John Smith took passage for England. In the years he'd been away from his native land, he had found not only the adventure he sought but also a measure of fame and fortune. He was returning with a coat of arms that gave him the right to call himself a gentleman, and a desire for even more adventure.

CHAPTER THREE

Preparations

It is easy to imagine John Smith in late 1604, standing on the deck of the ship that carried him back to England as it made its way up the River Thames from the open ocean to the great port of London. Sun-browned and hardened by battle and by long months in slavery, he must have stood at the ship's rail and gazed with a mixture of joy and gratitude at the sight of his homeland.

We know from a portrait of John Smith made later in his life that he was a ruggedly handsome man with curly hair. He wore his beard squared off, rather than pointed in the fashion of the day. In that portrait, Smith stands with his right hand cocked on his hip and his left hand on the hilt of his sword as if he is ready to unsheathe it. His gaze seems to challenge the viewer. He had the look of a man who was sure of himself, cocky, ready to grab the world by the throat and squeeze until he got his way.

In 1604, as his ship neared London's center, Smith would have seen Greenwich Palace, the favorite residence of Queen Elizabeth I. No doubt he felt a sense of sadness and loss as he gazed at the graceful palace, for Elizabeth had died on March 24, 1603, while Smith was in Hungary.

The port of London was then, as now, one of the busiest in the world. A contemporary of Smith's described it this way: "A man would say, that seeth the shipping there, that it is [as if] a very wood of trees [had been] disbranched to make glades and let in light; so shaded it is with masts and sails."[1]

In addition to cargo and passenger vessels making their way to and from the wharves along the river's north bank, hundreds of narrow rowboats called "wherries"—water taxis that carried one or two passengers—crowded the river's surface. Swans, protected by law because their feathers were used to make pillows and comforters for the royal family, swam unafraid in the midst of all the river traffic.

As Smith looked over the busy river, he would have smiled as he heard the shouts of the rivermen and the cries of sailors working their vessels. After three years in Europe, the sounds of his native English tongue must have been like music to his ears.

As his ship slipped past the Tower of London, Smith may have caught sight of Sir Walter Raleigh. The romantic, dashing Sir Walter, one-time favorite of Queen Elizabeth, was at that time a prisoner in the ancient white castle that for many years served as a jail, and he often walked on the tower's ramparts overlooking the Thames.

Soon after passing the tower, John Smith's ship would have found a mooring, perhaps within sight of London Bridge. In 1604, the bridge was already more than four centuries old. Its stone arches stretched almost one thousand feet across the Thames to join the city's heart to the south bank of the river. It was (and still would be if it had not been torn down early in the nineteenth century) an architectural wonder. Both sides of the narrow road that ran down the middle of the bridge were crowded with shops topped by houses, including some that were seven stories high.

Exactly what Smith did after he stepped ashore in England is not certain. He was rich, at least for a yeoman's son from a tiny farming village. The £500 he had been awarded by Prince Bathory for his service in Hungary and his later imprisonment was equal to about $40,000 in today's money. No doubt one of the first things he did was to buy new clothes. To be fashionable, he would have dressed in a richly embroidered silk doublet (jacket), topped by a pleated collar called a ruff, along with fancy breeches, silk stockings decorated with gold or silver, and a colorful velvet cloak. At his waist he would have worn a dagger and a sword.

A stranger in London, John Smith almost certainly took lodgings in one of the city's many taverns. There he found not only shelter but also good English beef and ale, and companions who must have listened with wonder to his tales of adventure.

Perhaps Smith visited the Globe Theatre, where William Shakespeare's *Othello* was being staged. In the audience he no doubt joined the "groundlings" that stood before the raised stage and cheered and jeered the actors (there were no actresses) in a way that would shock modern theatergoers.

As Smith socialized in London, we can be sure he heard excited talk about plans that were afoot to establish settlements in the New World of America. This was just the kind of talk that would attract his attention.

To be sure, by Smith's time English ships had been visiting the coast of North America for more than a century. John Cabot, an Italian sailing under the English flag, was the first of these visitors, arriving in the waters off Newfoundland just a few years after Christopher Columbus "discovered" the Americas. He was followed by other explorers, then by a steady stream of fishing vessels who found the seas off what is now New England thick with cod.

But the English, involved in a series of costly wars in Europe during those years, gave little thought to colonizing the New World. As a consequence, Spain, which was then the strongest and richest nation in the world, was able to enjoy a virtual colonial monopoly in both North and South America.

It wasn't until 1584 that the English made their first serious attempt to establish a colony in America. In that year, Raleigh (the same Sir Walter who was languishing in the Tower of London when John Smith sailed past in 1604) obtained a royal grant to settle the huge territory between French-controlled Canada and the lands the Spanish called La Florida. He named that territory Virginia in honor of Queen Elizabeth, the Virgin Queen.

In 1585, Raleigh made his first attempt to settle the land he called Virginia. That attempt failed within a few months. In 1587, he tried again, sending more than one hundred settlers, including women and children, to Roanoke, a small island just off the shore of what is now North Carolina. The group, led by a painter named John White, was able to establish a small settlement on Roanoke, but it soon ran short of food and other supplies.

Reluctantly, White returned to England to obtain provisions. His timing could not have been worse for, while he was in London in 1588, the Spanish sent a great armada to attack England. Virtually every ship in the nation was pressed into service to drive the Spanish off, and White was not able to return to Roanoke until 1590. By that time all the settlers he'd left behind had disappeared. Among the missing were White's daughter, son-in-law, and a baby girl named Virginia Dare, the first English child born in America. To this day, the fate of these settlers remains a mystery.

While Raleigh failed in his attempts to establish a colony in Virginia, English enthusiasm for the idea remained strong. By 1604, when John Smith returned from the wars against the Turks, "certaine of the Nobilitie, Gentrie, and Merchants"[2] were busy making plans to establish several settlements along America's eastern shore.

While we don't know exactly how John Smith became involved in these plans, we do know that early in 1605 he joined a group of influential and wealthy Englishmen who had petitioned King James I for a patent (legal document) giving

From left to right, the Susan Constant, Godspeed, *and*
Discovery. *The original painting by Griffith Bailey Coale hangs
in the Virginia State Capitol Building in Richmond. The three
ships left the port of London in 1606 with the hope of founding a
new colony in Virginia.*

them the right to establish a colony in Virginia. This group
included Richard Hakluyt, a famous geographer and writer
who chronicled the exploits of many early explorers and
colonists; Edward Maria Wingfield, a well-born, forty-year-old
ex-soldier who was one of "the first movers"[3] of the Virginia
colony; Christopher Newport, an experienced sailor who eventually commanded the vessels that carried the settlers to
Virginia; and Captain Bartholomew Gosnold, who had earlier
attempted to establish a colony in New England.

Obtaining a charter (or patent) to settle in the New World was a time-consuming and expensive business. According to Smith, he eventually invested "more than five hundred pound of (his) owne estate" in the plan to establish the Virginia settlement.[4]

We can be sure that John Smith also invested his time. From a letter written by Henry Hudson in 1610, it seems certain that Smith established contact with the famous sailor and navigator, perhaps to learn about mapmaking, an art at which Hudson was adept.

Finally, on April 10, 1606, King James I affixed his seal to a royal charter granting Hakluyt, Gosnold, and the others the right to settle in the New World. According to this charter, there were to be two joint-stock companies (something like public companies that today are listed on the New York Stock Exchange) responsible for colonizing the huge territory of Virginia.

One of these, known as the Plymouth Company of Virginia, was responsible for settling northern Virginia, roughly the area we know today as New England. The second, known as the London Company of Virginia, was responsible for the settling of the area that lay between Cape Fear, North Carolina, and the mouth of the Hudson River. A royal council of thirteen men named by the king would watch over the activities of both companies. The actual day-to-day governing of the settlements would be left to councils chosen by the parent companies.

Once Gosnold and the other patentees had their charter in hand, their work began in earnest. Crossing the Atlantic Ocean in 1606 with settlers and sufficient food, weapons, building materials, and other supplies to build a city in the wilderness was a complex and costly undertaking. For eight months, the leaders of the Virginia expedition were busy raising money; obtaining food for the voyage and supplies to begin their settlement; drawing up instructions for the settlers; recruiting sailors, ships' officers, and settlers; and attending to what must have seemed like a million details. By his own account, Smith was deeply involved in these preparations. While he does not give us any details, it would have been natural for a man with his military experience to act as a recruiter. It would have been his job to enlist men able to stand up to the rigors of establishing a settlement, men who could fire a musket and swing a sword in case of trouble with the Indians of Virginia.

Eventually, the patentees obtained three ships. The largest of these was the *Susan Constant*. Though it was the flagship of the fleet that would carry the colonists to Virginia, it was only about 70 feet (21 meters) in length, or slightly larger than a modern luxury yacht. The other vessels were the *Godspeed*, about 40 feet (13 meters) in length, and the *Discovery*, a type of vessel known as a pinnace, which was about 30 feet (9 meters) long. All three of these vessels were three masted, with square sails on their main- and fore-masts and lateen sails (something like the sails on a modern sailboat) on their rearmost, or mizzen, masts.

These three small ships were to carry, by John Smith's count, a total of 105 colonists—along with an unknown number of sailors and officers, plus food and other supplies—some three thousand miles across the open ocean.

Why would John Smith join this expedition? Why would he leave England to travel an immense distance across a hostile ocean in the hope of building a settlement in the wild, untamed wilderness of the New World?

Obviously, Smith hoped to find adventure. His thirst for excitement had only been temporarily slaked in Hungary. The knight-errant was ready to joust again. At the same time, like all the colonists, he must have hoped to find riches in Virginia. For years, Spain and Portugal had taken unbelievable wealth from South and Central America and Mexico. The English believed that they, too, would find untold riches in the New World.

Though there had never been any reliable report that the region was rich with gold, this belief was so prevalent that reference was made to Virginia's riches in the popular play *Eastward Ho!*, produced in 1605. "Golde is more plentifull [in Virginia]," one character in the play remarks, "then copper is with us; . . . Why, man, all their dripping-pans and their chamber-potts are pure gould . . . ; all the prisoners they take are fetered in gold; and for rubies and diamonds they goe forth on holydayes and gather 'hem by the sea-shore to hang on their childrens coates, and sticke in their children's caps. . . ."[5]

Smith would also have been motivated by patriotism and by his strong Protestant faith, a faith that is obvious in much of what he wrote. As a good Protestant subject of his king, he wanted the English empire to expand and grow stronger. He hoped to convert the Indians of the region to Protestant Christianity, and to establish new markets for goods made in England.

Smith may have had another, more personal motive, as well. He may have felt he had to act quickly if he was ever going to achieve higher rank. Though only twenty-five years of age when he first heard of the Virginia colony, in his time he was considered a middle-aged man. The philosopher Francis Bacon, who lived at about the same time as Smith, said of himself in 1592, "I was now somewhat ancient: one and thirty years is a great deal of sand in the hour glass."[6] If Smith felt the way Bacon did—"somewhat ancient"—he must have been anxious to leave England to start the next great adventure of his life.

In mid-December of 1606, Smith may have joined with Gosnold and Wingfield and Captain Newport and the other leaders of the Virginia venture on board Drake's ship, the *Golden Hind*. It was traditional, in those days, for adventurers bound for America to dine on board the vessel Drake had sailed around the world before setting sail. If such a dinner took place, toasts were no doubt drunk to King James I and to the success of their plans. Perhaps Smith or one of the others quoted an ode written by the poet Michael Drayton not long before they set sail:

> To get the Pearle and Gold,
> And ours to hold,
> VIRGINIA
> Earth's onely paradise. . . .[7]

With the banquet and the toasts out of the way and all preparations made, the expedition was ready to depart. On December 19, Smith and the other colonists climbed on board the three ships of the Virginia-bound fleet. Early the next morning, the ships weighed anchor and made their way to the open ocean. John Smith was about to begin the greatest adventure of his life, the adventure that would gain him lasting fame.

CHAPTER FOUR

The Voyage

As soon as the three Virginia-bound ships left their anchorage in the Thames they ran into bad luck. The wind—favorable when they started to slip down the river—shifted so that it was blowing from dead ahead. By the time the *Susan Constant*, *Godspeed*, and *Discovery* made their way into the waters of the North Sea they were sailing into the teeth of a winter gale.

For more than a month, the vessels were forced to lie at anchor with their sails furled in a region known as the Downs, just off the coast of Kent about 75 miles (120 kilometers) from London. As the vessels lay ahull, they pitched and yawed cease-lessly. Battered by huge rollers, they strained at their anchors, their timbers groaning as the fearsome wind wailed in their rig-ging like a thousand banshees.

It is almost impossible to imagine the misery endured by the people on the three tiny vessels as they lay anchored off the coast of England. The sailors and a few of the settlers who had been at sea before, including Smith, probably bore up well. Most of those bound for Virginia, however, were landlubbers. In fact, though they lived on an island, most had never even seen the sea before. They suffered terribly from seasickness and, worse, from the terror of the unfamiliar.

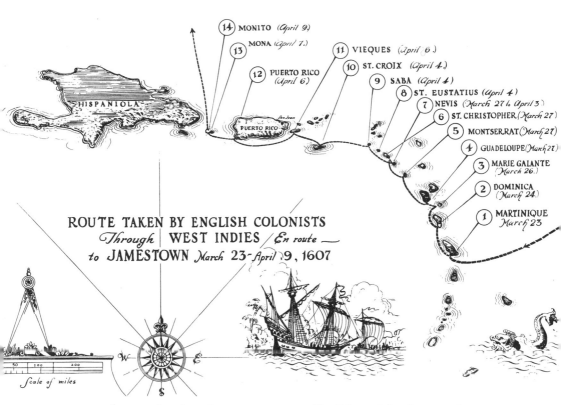

A map showing the many stops at Caribbean islands to explore and trade before the Susan Constant, Godspeed, *and* Discovery *continued north to Virginia.*

No one on the vessels was more miserable than the Reverend Robert Hunt, an Anglican minister who had been recruited to serve as the company's preacher. According to Smith, Hunt "was so weake and sicke, that few expected his recovery."[1]

As sick as he was, though, Hunt was not robbed of his courage. Advised by others on the ships to quit the expedition, he refused to go ashore, even though his home was just a few miles from the wintry coast he could see from the ship's deck when he wasn't busy vomiting over the rail.

By John Smith's count, about half of the 105 passengers were so-called gentlemen. In other words, they were of a higher social standing than the fifty-five commoners whose blood was not quite so blue.

The gentlemen on the vessels included Edward Maria Wingfield, one of the highest-born members of the company; George Percy, the son of the earl of Northumberland; and the Reverend Hunt. The captains of the three ships—Christopher Newport of the *Susan Constant*, Bartholomew Gosnold of the *Godspeed*, and John Ratcliffe in command of the *Discovery*—were also gentlemen. Smith, while considered a gentleman because of his coat of arms, must have been looked upon with suspicion by the highborn members of the company. Birth, to these men, was much more important than accomplishments.

English society in the seventeenth century was intensely class-conscious. Even in church, different social levels were segregated. Men who were considered high-born sat at the front of the church with their families; those lower born sat behind them; and the commoners—yeomen and tradesmen and tenant farmers—stood respectfully behind the pews. And once each year, all English churchgoers (and that was virtually everybody in England) heard a homily extolling the virtues of knowing one's place in an orderly society:

> Almighty God hath created and appointed all things in heaven, earth and waters in a most excellent and perfect order. . . ." that homily declared. "In earth, he hath assigned kings, princes, with other governors under them, all in good and necessary order. . . . Some are in high degree, some in low, some kings and princes, some inferiors and subjects, priests and laymen, masters and servants, fathers and children, husbands and wives, rich and poor, and every one have need of the other. . . .[2]

Given the terrible conditions on the ships as they waited for the winds to turn favorable and the seas to settle, it was natural for tempers to grow short. Storm-tossed and forced to suffer in idleness in cramped, damp quarters reeking of vomit for hour after hour, the passengers soon began bickering among themselves.

In all likelihood, Wingfield was among those involved in whatever arguments and dissension broke out as the ships lay at anchor. He is remembered as a snob who was "puffed up by his own sense of superior birth and position."[3]

Finally, after a delay of almost six weeks, the winds turned fair. The three little ships with their miserable passengers headed into the open ocean. While those on board were undoubtedly relieved to be under way, some among their number, including Smith, must have wondered what terrors lay ahead. During the long delay much of the food and drink that had been taken on board to keep the settlers alive during their early days in Virginia had already been consumed.

Still, the settlers must have been filled with hope as the ships made their slow way to the west, leaving England in their wake. After all, hadn't the backers of the colonial expedition promised them an easy life, surrounded by friendly natives who would be happy to see them come, ready and willing to trade gold and gems for baubles?

Captain Newport, a veteran of several Atlantic crossings who had lost one arm in a fight with the Spanish, followed the safest—though not the shortest or fastest—route across the three thousand miles of open ocean between England and Virginia. Instead of going straight across the ocean where the little fleet would have struggled against the North Atlantic's fearsome winter storms, he sailed south by southwest to the Canary Islands, about 200 miles (322 kilometers) off the coast of Africa. This first leg of the ocean voyage was uneventful except for "a blazing Starre" (a comet) the sailors and settlers saw arc across the sky on the night of February 12.[4]

Many who saw the comet's passage that night must have shuddered. In those days, heavenly phenomena such as comets and eclipses were considered omens that something terrible was about to happen. And indeed, given the hardship and starvation and death that lay ahead for so many of the settlers on the three tiny ships, perhaps the comet was the omen of doom it was believed to be.

Around March 1, almost two and a half months after leaving London—and about the time Smith and the other colonists had reasonably expected to be erecting their settlement in Virginia—the ships reached the Canary Islands. After taking on water for the voyage ahead, they departed.

Somehow—and it is not at all clear exactly what happened from his writings—John Smith was in trouble by the time the *Susan Constant, Godspeed,* and *Discovery* left the Canaries. According to witnesses, he was "restrained as a prisoner, upon the scandalous suggestions of some . . . who [believed] he intended to usurp the government . . . and make himself king."[5]

While we don't know exactly what happened to result in Smith's arrest, it seems likely that he and Edward Maria Wingfield locked horns over some matter. Perhaps Wingfield ordered Smith around as if he were a servant. Perhaps Smith—who was never afraid to speak his mind—openly disagreed with Wingfield or, just as likely, bragged a bit too much about his exploits as a soldier in Hungary.

If, indeed, Wingfield was angry with Smith, it would have been perfectly in character for the nobleman to name him as a traitor, even if on its face the accusation seemed silly. In those days, naming an enemy as a plotter was a favored way, especially among the highborn, of dealing with someone troublesome. Even a hint of disloyalty or of plotting against lawful authority was enough to get a man (or woman, for that matter) hanged or locked away for years.

Whatever happened, Smith was "restrained" when the three ships set sail from the Canaries. If he wasn't locked up, he was at least limited in terms of his freedom and would remain so for about thirteen weeks.

During that time, the vessels crossed the Atlantic, arriving at the Caribbean island of Martinique on March 21. From there, the ships island-hopped along the curving archipelago of the West Indies, calling at Dominica and Guadeloupe, then slipping past Montserrat to drop anchor at the tiny island of Nevis.

The islands gave the men in the expedition—including Smith, unless he was physically forced to remain on shipboard—much needed opportunities to relax and stretch their legs on shore. George Percy described them as "very faire . . . the Trees full of sweet and good smels. . . ."

Percy also provided history with one of its most complete word-portraits of the Indians of the West Indies. "Their bodies," he wrote, "are all painted red to keepe away the biting of Muscetos [mosquitoes]. They goe all naked without covering. The haire of their head is a yard long, all of a length, pleated . . . (and) hanging down to their wastes."[6]

On the island of Guadeloupe, the colonists again went ashore. There they found a natural hot spring that was, according to Percy, "so hot that no man was able to stand long by it." Captain Newport, he added, "caused a piece of Porke to be put in it; which boyled it so, in the space of halfe an hour, as no fire could [improve] it."[7]

By the time the fleet anchored at Nevis, Smith was in such disfavor with some of the leaders of the expedition, Wingfield included, that they tried to execute him on the beach. In his history of the voyage, Smith says they built a gallows, but "Captain Smith . . . could not be perswaded to use them."[8]

This simple sentence may be one of the great understatements of history. It is easy to imagine John Smith, captain of cavalry, victor of single-handed combat with three Turkish champions, standing on the beach, armed with a brace of pistols and a cutlass, daring those who wanted to punish him to take him to the gallows.

Not surprisingly, the other settlers decided to let Smith live.

Eventually, the ships made their way to the Virgin Islands, where they anchored. From there, the fleet headed north, calling at Mona between Puerto Rico and Santo Domingo, then known as Hispaniola. One of the settlers, a gentleman named Edward Brookes, died while exploring Mona. It must have been terribly hot in the islands, at least for an Englishman not used to tropic heat and humidity, for Brookes died, George Percy wrote, when his "fat melted within him, by the great heate and drought of the Countrey."9

On April 10, the Virginia-bound ships left the West Indies behind and sailed north, making use of the north-setting current of the Gulf Stream to speed them on their way at about 5 miles per hour. Soon they began anxiously looking for the land that was their goal.

About ten days later, as the ships reached a point where, by Captain Newport's reckoning, they should have been off the coast of Virginia, they were struck by one of the gales that regularly roar across the Gulf Stream. They were forced by the storm to "heave to," with their sails shortened and bows turned to the wind.

On April 22 the storm passed. For the next three days, Newport searched in vain for some sight of land. As time passed, some of the settlers became afraid they were lost. John Ratcliffe, captain of the smallest of the three ships, was all for turning tail and heading for England and safety.

Finally, at four in the morning of April 26, as the sun was just beginning to rise above the eastern horizon, land was sighted. It was the southern point of land guarding the entry to the Chesapeake Bay—the exact place they'd hoped to make landfall. According to Smith, who believed along with most of his contemporaries that the Creator had a hand in all human affairs, "God the guider of all good actions . . . did drive them by his providence to their desired Port, beyond all their expectations. . . ."10

Soon, as the sun rose in the eastern sky over a world none on the ships had ever seen, the *Susan Constant*, the *Godspeed*, and the *Discovery* sailed into the broad mouth of the Chesapeake.

CHAPTER FIVE

"A Fruitfull and Delightsome Land"

The sun was low in the eastern sky as the three ships carrying Smith and the other Virginia settlers eased their way into the broad, uncharted expanse of the Chesapeake Bay. The small fleet's flagship, the *Susan Constant*, led the way with the smaller *Godspeed* and *Discovery* following in her wake like ducklings after their mother. As the vessels edged into the bay, Captain Newport stood on the *Constant*'s high stern deck, searching for a safe anchorage.

At a shouted order from Newport, the helmsman who stood belowdeck steering the ship leaned against the whipstaff that controlled the vessel's rudder. The *Susan Constant*'s bow turned into the wind as sailors aloft quickly furled her sails. The other ships followed suit and soon, with the loud rattle of anchor chains, the fleet came to rest near the bay's southern shore.

As the tattered vessels bobbed at anchor, the settlers, anxious to feel solid land underfoot again, crowded the ships' rails. They stared excitedly and nervously at the shore, wondering what adventures and dangers lay in wait in this place that was so alien and unknown to them.

The land these Englishmen saw was low-lying and swampy. Close to shore, the marshy terrain was thick with reeds and cat-tails and tangled underbrush. Further inland, away from the brackish water of the bay, the swamp turned to a thick forest of pine, oak, walnut, and cedar trees, some as tall as 80 feet (24 meters) and hung with vines as thick as a grown man's thigh.

It was springtime when the English sailed into the Chesapeake. Soft, cool breezes heavy with the perfume of flowers and wild strawberries that were just ripening and with the thick smell of the forest itself blew across the ships as they rocked gently at anchor. These fragrant breezes gave the set-tlers no hint of the terrible heat and humidity that would settle on the Chesapeake as spring turned to summer. Nor did the breezes give any hint of the sickness that would kill so many of the English colonists before that summer ended.

Perhaps a raccoon or muskrat came to the water's edge while the settlers watched, for the land was filled with game, just as the waters of the bay were filled with fish. John Smith, writing later, told how the bay teemed with mullet, eels, perch, sea trout, sturgeon as long as a man is tall, and a creature he described as "the most strange fish . . . so like the picture of . . . a dragon, as possibl[y] can be."[1] In addition to this "dragon," possibly a sea horse, the settlers found the bay full of shellfish, including shrimp, oysters, and crabs so large that just one could feed four people.

We can be sure that as those on the ships stared hungrily at what Smith called a "fruitfull and delightsome land,"[2] they were themselves being carefully watched by Indians who hid in the tall grass or in the forest, waiting to see what the bearded strangers on the ships would do.

The Indians who lived in the region around the bay were members of the Algonkian family of Indian tribes. They were ruled by a powerful chief named Powhatan. These people, called the Powhatan, lived as their ancestors had lived for thousands of years. They had no metal tools or implements. They had never discovered the wheel. They farmed with tools of stone and wood, hunted with bows and bone- or flint-tipped arrows, and caught fish in nets of plaited reeds.

Powhatan—who had changed his name from Wahunsonacock when he became chief of the Powhatan people, some time about 1570—was a ruthless, cunning, and often cruel leader. When he first became chief, or *werowance*, he was the ruler of just a few hundred people. By 1607, however, he was the despotic king of about nine thousand who inhabited much of Tidewater Virginia (the region around the Chesapeake) and part of coastal North Carolina. A tyrant, he demanded 80 percent of all the skins his people trapped, the fish they caught and dried, the crops they raised, and the pearls they harvested. He was also a fierce warrior who would do anything to protect his kingdom and his riches.

For many years before Smith and the other settlers arrived in the Chesapeake region, tribal priests had prophesied that Powhatan's lands would be overrun by invaders who would come from the east. To protect himself from these invaders, Powhatan virtually wiped out the Chesapeake Indians who lived between his main village and the eastern coast of Virginia. It is very likely that he was also responsible for the extermination of what is known today as the so-called "Lost Colony" of English settlers at Roanoke, North Carolina.

While John Smith and the other English settlers knew the region around the Chesapeake was inhabited by Indians, and while they fully expected some conflicts with the natives, they had no idea that a man like Powhatan would oppose them as they struggled to establish an English outpost in the New World. Even if they had known, however, the English settlers would have been undeterred. They were every bit as determined to build their colony in Virginia as Powhatan was to keep them out.

The English, meanwhile, wasted little time before going ashore. Almost immediately after the ships dropped anchor, about twenty-five men made their way to the beach near the point of land that guards the southern entrance to the Chesapeake, a point of land they named Cape Henry in honor of the eldest son of King James I. The point of land opposite it, on the other side of the Chesapeake's mouth, they named Cape Charles, in honor of the prince who would become King Charles I of England.

Smith, still "restrained" because of the charges brought against him early in the voyage, was not included in the landing party that went ashore on April 26. It is easy to imagine him pacing the *Susan Constant*'s deck impatiently as Percy, Newport, Wingfield, Gosnold, Gabriel Archer, and about twenty other men made their way to the beach.

By the time the party headed ashore, the sun was high. The men must have been uncomfortable in their heavy English clothing and the armor breastplates and helmets they wore as protection in case of an attack. They also must have been nervous, for none of them really knew what to expect. Many of the English thought the Indians were cannibals waiting to attack at the first opportunity and that lions, or maybe even dragons, lived in the forest.

George Percy, who wrote the most detailed account of this first exploration, was delighted by what he described as "faire meddowes and goodly tall Trees; with such Fresh-waters running through the woods, as I was almost ravished at the first sight thereof."[3]

On this first day ashore, the settlers did little more than reconnoiter. No doubt they kept a sharp lookout for Indians. As they explored, however, they saw no signs of any of the natives who lived in the region.

That evening, however, as the shore party was preparing to return to the ships, Indians, possibly some of the surviving members of the Chesapeake tribe, crept from the woods "like Beares," in Percy's words, "with their Bowes in their mouths." Once close enough, the Indians—there were only five or six—loosed a volley of arrows at the settlers. Gabriel Archer was wounded in both hands, and a sailor, Matthew Morton, "in two places of the body very dangerous[ly]," according to Percy.[4] The English responded with a volley of musket shot that drove the Indians back into the woods.

This brief encounter on the beach near what is now Newport, Virginia, was a foreshadowing of what was to come in the years that followed. The Powhatan people and the settlers the Indians called "the coat-wearing people"[5] clashed time and time again, seemingly bent on outdoing each other in terms of their bloodthirsty behavior.

At that time, though, both sides were content to retreat— the Indians to the cover of the thick forests, the English to the safety of their ships.

That night, sealed boxes—one on each of the three ships— were opened. These boxes had been sent with the settlers by the Virginia Company with orders that they be opened as soon as the colonists reached Virginia. Inside each box was a list of the men the company had chosen to lead the colony. The company officials had wanted the names kept secret until the sea voyage was over so that none of those chosen to lead would be tempted to challenge Captain Newport's leadership while the ships were in mid-ocean.

Many of the gentlemen on the vessels undoubtedly expected to be chosen to lead. As the names were read, these men, used to high positions in England, must have held their breath expectantly. On the list were seven names: Edward Maria Wingfield, Captain Newport, Bartholomew Gosnold, John Ratcliffe, John Martin, George Kendall—all high-born gentlemen. The seventh name was John Smith, the farmer's son from Lincolnshire.

Smith was undoubtedly proud to learn that he had been named one of the leaders of the Virginia venture. Of course, he had led men in battle, but this was different. Now he was one of the leaders of a great and exciting attempt to transplant England's military power and culture to the New World. Adding spice to his accomplishment, no doubt, was the fact

In his journal, George Percy wrote, "And in that place was the Box opened, wherin the Counsell for Virginia was nominated. . . ."

that he had been chosen to lead men—men like Percy and others among the gentlemen—who would not even acknowledge him with a nod on the streets of London. Smith's pride must soon have turned to bitterness, though, when it became clear that Wingfield and others on the council had no intention of letting him assume his position of leadership. In fact, during the weeks immediately following the colonists' arrival in Virginia, Smith remained an outcast.

During those weeks, the settlers put together a shallop, a small boat that had been carried to Virginia in pieces. Then, without any help from Smith, they went in search of a place to establish their settlement. During their explorations they had frequent and friendly contact with Indians who were anxious to trade food for baubles and trinkets they'd never seen before.

On May 13, the settlers chose a spot on the north bank of the broad river the Indians called the Powhatan (renamed the James by the English) as the site of their settlement. The spot they chose was a peninsula about 3 miles (5 kilometers) long and 1 mile wide that projected into the river. Roughly shaped like a comma, this peninsula was linked to the northern shore by a narrow neck of land that could easily be defended. (This narrow link to the mainland, which was under water at high tide in 1607, has since been washed away by the river, turning the peninsula into an island.)

At first, the English called this tiny European outpost in the wilderness James Fort, in honor of the English king. As the settlement slowly grew with the passage of time, it became known as James Towne and later, Jamestown.

Though John Smith and the other settlers had no way of knowing it, this toehold on the eastern seaboard of the vast North American continent was to be the first successful English settlement in the New World. And John Smith, the outcast who was at first not even allowed to go ashore, would prove to be the man most responsible for its success.

CHAPTER SIX

"A Verie Fit Place . . ."

On May 13, the *Susan Constant, Godspeed,* and *Discovery* were moved from their anchorage near the mouth of the Chesapeake to a spot just off the place we know today as Jamestown Island. The deepwater channel swept close to the shore at that spot, so close that the settlers were able to moor the three ships to trees on the beach.

The next day, Smith and the other settlers, helped by the sailors, unloaded the ships. Building materials, tents for shelter, food and drink, livestock, tools, trade goods, everything needed to survive in the wilderness was carried ashore.

The settlers had precise directions from the Virginia Company telling them exactly what to look for when choosing a location for their settlement. According to these instructions, they were to find a location on a river far enough from the ocean to provide some protection against surprise attack. The river on which they built their settlement was to be deep enough to allow large vessels to carry supplies to the settlement. This river was to bend to the northwest, for in that way the settlers would easily be able to find passage to "the other sea"—the Pacific Ocean—and the riches of the Orient.

On May 14, Smith and the other men selected the site for their new colony. It was easy to defend and close to the river, but so swampy that mosquitoes became a real health issue.

In addition, they were to find a spot that was "the strongest, most wholesome and fertile place."[1] The place chosen was to be uninhabited by Indians, and no native people were to live between the settlement and the sea. Finally—and this was to have a great impact on the way the settlement was built at first—the instructions ordered the settlers to "have great care not to offend the naturals."[2]

To this day, there is a great deal of debate about the wisdom of the choice of the Jamestown site for the settlement. There's no denying that it was not a very "wholesome and fertile" plot of land. About half the peninsula was swamp covered by mud and marsh grass. This was a perfect breeding ground for mosquitoes and, hence, for disease. The remaining land was, for the most part, heavily timbered forest not particularly suitable for farming.

The most important consideration, however, at least as far as the settlers were concerned, was their ability to defend themselves from attacks by the Indians and by the Spanish. Though Spain and England had signed a treaty of peace in 1604, the English were worried that the Spanish would drive them from the New World. Jamestown may have been low and swampy, but it was ideally situated at a place where lookouts could spot approaching ships in plenty of time to allow the settlers to mount a defense. At the same time, its geography afforded natural protection not only against Spanish vessels but against Indian attacks.

While John Smith was still in disfavor with Wingfield and some of the other leaders of the Virginia venture, his advice was undoubtedly sought by those leaders as they decided where to establish the settlement. He was, after all, a soldier who had won fame and fortune in battle. He knew about building defensive positions and had seen wooden forts in Eastern Europe. Smith, for his part, considered Jamestown "a verie fit place for the erecting of a great cittie."[3]

Before any work began on the settlement itself, the members of the ruling council—excluding Smith, of course, who was still being ostracized—were sworn in as the colony's leaders. After they took their oaths of office, probably administered by the Reverend Hunt, the council members elected Wingfield the colony's first president.

After the swearing in, the spot the settlers had chosen to establish their colony became a beehive of activity. "Now falleth every man to worke," one of the settlers later reported, "the Councell contrive (design) the Fort, the rest cut downe trees to make place to pitch their Tents, some provide clapbord to relade the ships; some make gardens, some nets, &c."[4]

While there's no doubt the Englishmen set right to work, there's also no doubt that the above statement is an exaggeration. It isn't at all likely that this wide range of activities—chopping down trees and fashioning clapboard to fill the ships' holds for the return voyage, making nets and planting gardens while erecting shelters and working on a fort—were all carried on at the same time and on the first day ashore.

The first order of business was, we can be sure, erecting some kind of defense against Indian attacks. After all, it had only been a matter of a few days since the first shore party was attacked on the beach near the mouth of the Chesapeake. Wingfield, however, remembering the Virginia Company's instructions to do nothing that would "offend the naturals," ordered only that a small breastwork of tree limbs, shaped roughly like a half-moon, be thrown together for protection.

While this half-moon shaped jumble of tree limbs was being constructed, other settlers cleared an area near the fortification where tents could be raised. This task was made simpler by the fact that the English had, apparently without realizing it, chosen as the site of their wilderness settlement a spot that had once been the location of an Indian village or hunting camp. That made the business of clearing the land easier than it might have been, since any trees on the site were relatively small and easy to chop down.

Soon, the settlers raised the tents that were to serve as James Towne's earliest dwellings. These tents, the only real shelter the settlers had for several months, had been purchased for the colonists' use by the Virginia Company. To save money, the company bought supplies that were probably used in the Netherlands. In fact, these tents were so old that they were half-rotten even before they were raised by the settlers in Virginia.

As shaky as this beginning was, it was still a beginning. Within a matter of just a few days, James Towne started to take shape on the shores of the little peninsula.

As the settlers established this toehold in the wilderness, John Smith must have been determined to do everything possible to gain what he considered his rightful place as a leader of the other men. Somehow, Smith gained Captain Newport's confidence. On May 21, just eight days after the English moved their ships to Jamestown, Smith was chosen to accompany the captain and about twenty other men on a journey of exploration up the James River in search of either gold or a passage to the Pacific Ocean.

George Percy described the James as "one of the famousest Rivers that ever was found by any Christian . . . where ships of great burthen may harbour in safetie." As the explorers made their way up the river, he added, they saw "the goodliest Woods as Beech, Oke, Cedar, Cypresse, Wal-nuts, Sassafras, and Vines in great abundance . . . , and other Trees unknowne; and all the grounds bespred with many sweet and delicate flowres of divers colours and kindes." The woods were rich with fruit including strawberries, mulberries, and raspberries; and the river itself was thick with "fish of all kindes." There were, Percy said, "great and laarge Medowes" that would make good pastureland for cattle as well as a large number of "Deere both Red and Fallow" along with "Beares, Foxes, Otters, Bevers, Muskats, and wild beasts unknown."[5]

On May 23, the settlers met eight Indians in a canoe. According to Captain Gabriel Archer, one of the explorers, an Indian named Navirans used his foot to draw a picture of the river in the soil. Provided with pen and paper by Archer, "he layd out the whole River from the [Chesapeake] bay to the end of it so farr as passadg[e] was for boats. . . . "[6] He also agreed to guide the Englishmen on their journey.

With Navirans showing the way, the settlers soon made their way to an impassable series of waterfalls not far from the present-day site of Richmond. There they were entertained by a chief they thought was Powhatan, but who was actually one of the great chief's sons. Though Smith and the others wanted to continue exploring on foot, this chief convinced them that they should turn back, probably because he was concerned that they might establish friendly contact with the Monacan Indians, enemies of the Powhatans, who lived north of the falls.

Having been turned back at the falls, Newport, Smith, and the others returned to James Towne. The return journey took several days as the explorers stopped at several villages where they were entertained with feasts and songs and dances. In the village of Appomattox, they met a female *werowance*, or tribal chief. (A *werowance* could be either male or female.) Archer described this *werowance* as a nearly naked, "fatt lustie manly woman," adorned with copper jewelry, sporting a scowl that only disappeared when Captain Newport gave her gifts.[7]

On this voyage, they also met for the first time Openchancanough, Powhatan's younger brother and one of the most powerful of all the Powhatan Indians. As the settlers were to learn in later years, this chief, a wily and brave warrior, would pose a much greater threat to the English presence in Virginia than Powhatan ever did.

The party of explorers noticed that the Indians closer to James Towne were less friendly, more wary. Suddenly, on May 27, as they neared the settlement, Navirans, their guide, refused to accompany them any farther. Alarmed, Newport, Smith, and the others rushed back to the settlement as fast as they could.

There, they discovered that just one day earlier, several hundred Indians had attacked the half-moon "fort" that had been hastily thrown together on Wingfield's orders. In the attack, one boy and a man had been killed and at least ten men wounded by arrows. Wingfield himself was almost killed when an arrow passed through his beard but missed his body.

The settlement might well have ceased to exist right then. Luckily for the settlers, someone remembered that the *Susan Constant*, armed with cannon, was moored just a few feet off-shore. Quickly, the cannoneers on the ship were ordered to load one of the ship's big guns with what was known as "bar shot" and to fire at the Indians. When this shot—two cannon ball halves joined by a metal bar—crashed into the trees over the Indians' heads, the attackers fled.

This attack against the settlement was just the first of many. Men were attacked as they worked in the fields near the barricade or as they went into the woods to relieve themselves.

Finally, in the wake of these attacks, Wingfield decided to build something like a proper fort. Smith, who undoubtedly had advocated building a strong fort from the settlers' first days in James Towne, must have felt justified when, as one of the settlers later wrote, "the President was contented the Fort should be pallisadoed, the ordinance mounted, his men armed and exercised."[8]

During these early days in Virginia, Smith must have started acting more and more like a leader. It would have been natural for him at least to give advice—whether or not it was asked for. It would also have been natural for him to help build the fort and to leap into action during Indian attacks. His contributions to the settlement could not be overlooked. On June 10, he was finally sworn in as a member of James Towne's ruling council.

"So wel he demeaned himselfe in this busines, as all the company did see his innocencie . . . ," one of the settlers later wrote.[9] In reality, not "all the company" was in favor of Smith serving on the council or even wanted him to remain in Virginia. In fact, even on the day he was sworn in as a member of the council, some of the other leaders wanted to send him back to England so the Virginia Company could deal with him. Captain Newport and Reverend Hunt, however, somehow managed to convince the other leaders to allow Smith to take his place on the council.

How proud John Smith must have been when Wingfield and the other members of the council finally agreed to let him take his place as one of James Towne's leaders. He must have drawn himself up, thrown his shoulders back and his chest out, placed his right hand on the hilt of his sword or perhaps on a

*During the construction of the triangular fort,
the men continued to sleep in tents, while the ships lay moored
just offshore in the James River.*

Bible held out by Reverend Hunt, and raised his red-bearded chin high as he said the words of the oath. "I shall faithfully and truly declare my mind and opinion according to my heart and conscience in all things . . . " he said, the broad vowels of Elizabethan England rolling off his tongue as he pledged himself to the service of James Towne.[10]

No doubt John Smith was proud. To lead men in a dangerous undertaking and in a dangerous place, to serve England and his king—these were the great motivations of John Smith's life. As proud as he was, John Smith was fortunate that at that happy moment he had no way of knowing just how much suffering lay ahead for the colony, for the hundred or so men he'd sworn to serve, or for himself.

CHAPTER SEVEN

Plagued with Famine and Sickness

By June 15, 1607, the James Towne fort was completed. Built on the western end of what is now Jamestown Island, the triangular fort was constructed of logs placed side by side in a trench about 2 feet (.6 meter) deep and strengthened by crosspieces. The longest side, about 420 feet (128 meters) in length, faced the James River. The other sides were each about 300 feet (91 meters) long. At each corner of the palisade, the settlers built a round bulwark, or projection, where four or five cannon from the ships were mounted.

For many years it was believed the site of this fort had been eroded away by the James River in the four centuries since John Smith stepped ashore in Virginia. Recent excavations at Jamestown Island, however, have provided evidence that only a small corner of the fort's site has been lost to the ravages of time and the river.

The evidence uncovered in Virginia gives mute evidence to how hard John Smith and the other settlers worked in the summer of 1607, sweating and straining in unaccustomed heat and humidity to dig trenches, chop down trees, and build a palisade more than one thousand feet (305 meters) in total length. This task by itself would have kept them busy from dawn to dark, but they also had to load the *Susan Constant* and *Godspeed* with clapboard and other cargo for the return voyage to England, provide themselves with food and water, and stand guard against the increasingly unfriendly Indians.

On Monday, June 22, with the fort built, Captain Newport and his men departed for England, leaving the pinnace *Discovery* for the settlers to use for fishing and exploring. The *Susan Constant* and *Godspeed* were loaded not only with clapboard—then a valuable commodity in England—but also with ore thought to be rich with gold. Left behind in James Towne were some one hundred undersupplied, ill-equipped Englishmen.

As the ships raised their sails and headed downriver for the open ocean, the settlers must have gazed after them anxiously, longingly. Those who remained onshore had just enough food to last about thirteen weeks. They knew there was no way Newport could return before their food ran out.

The settlers, meanwhile, had done little to make themselves comfortable in the weeks since they stepped ashore. The palisade, of course, had been built and work had probably started on a storehouse in which grain and other supplies could be stored. This storehouse was fashioned of corner pilings placed in the ground like fence posts, covered with twigs and mud or clapboard. Its roof was made of reeds gathered from the swampy area near the settlement.

"[S]et your houses even and by a line, that your streets may have a good breadth, and be carried square about your market place . . . ," the leaders of the Virginia Company had written in their instructions for building the settlement.[1]

Instead, James Towne was little more than a rag-tag collection of half-rotten tents and what were known as "soldier holes"—shallow trenches in which men could sleep covered with branches or canvas to afford protection from the elements. A canvas awning stretched between two trees served as a church where Reverend Hunt preached from behind a podium fashioned from a log. An open trench served as the town's toilet, saving the settlers from having to go into the forest to relieve themselves at the risk of taking an arrow from an Indian hidden in the trees.

As bad as conditions were in the little settlement when Newport departed, however, they were to get much, much worse. Just days after his departure, the colonists were stricken with an epidemic, probably malaria or typhoid fever. At the same time, Indian attacks continued.

George Percy, the same gentleman who had been "ravished" at the first sight of Virginia, began writing what amounted to a death list.

"The sixt of August, there died John Asbie, of the bloudie Fl[u]x [dysentery]. The ninth day, died George Flowre, of the swelling. The tenth day, died William Bruster, Gentleman, of a wound given by the Savages. . . ." The list goes on and on. It includes the name of Bartholomew Gosnold, the brave and famous sea captain, who was, according to Percy, "honorably buried, having all the Ordnance in the Fort shot off, with many vollies of small shot."[2]

Smith fell ill, but recovered, as did all the others on the council except Gosnold. Indeed, in the hot summer months almost half the settlers died. "[T]he living," Smith wrote, "were scarce able to bury the dead."[3]

Percy, always ready with his quill and paper, left a moving account of those terrible days. "There were never Englishmen left in a forreigne Countrey in such miserie as wee were in this new discovered Virginia," he wrote. The men he called "feeble wretches" had only a handful of barley soaked in water to eat each day. Used to drinking good English beer, their only drink was river water, salty at high tide, filthy and full of slime at low tide.[4] So many were sick that only six men were able to keep watch against Indian attack.

"If there were any conscience in men, it would make their harts to bleed to heare the pitifull murmurings and out-cries of our sick men without releife, every night and day . . . some departing out of the World, many times three or foure in a night . . . ," Percy wrote. Careful to hide the fact that so many of them were dying, the colonists dragged the dead from their tents each morning, according to Percy, and buried them "like Dogges."[5]

In the midst of the disease and famine, James Towne was torn by internal conflict. George Kendall was the first casualty of this internal dissension, removed from the council because, Wingfield said, he "did practice to sowe discord between the President and Council."[6]

But the trouble didn't end there. On September 10, just as the dying began to slow, Ratcliffe, Martin, and Smith—the only remaining members of the original council—visited Wingfield in his tent and told him they had voted to remove him from his office as president of Virginia and as a member of the governing council.

In response, Wingfield warned Smith and the others that the instructions from the Virginia Company required a vote of the majority of thirteen councilors to remove him from office. Since only seven, including himself, had been named and Gosnold was now dead, there was no circumstance under which he could be voted out of office. Smith and the others promptly told him they would take the consequences of their actions and placed him under guard in the *Discovery*, anchored in the river just offshore.

Several times during the next few days, Wingfield was brought ashore to answer a variety of charges, including a claim that he took food from the common store for his own use and that he had planned to steal the pinnace and sail in it with some companions to Newfoundland. In reality, Wingfield's biggest crime was that he was an obnoxious, overbearing snob (as were many men and women of his class and in his time). As a snob, though, he was a perfect target for colonists who were looking for someone—anyone—to blame for all their problems. According to Smith, by the time he was kicked out of office, Wingfield had "ordred the affaires in such sort that he was generally hated [by] all" in the colony.[7]

Ultimately, Wingfield claimed his right as a highborn Englishman to have his case tried in England. Sent back to the pinnace under guard, he was replaced as president by Captain John Ratcliffe.

During this period Wingfield was forced to answer to John Smith's charge that he, Wingfield, had unjustly accused him of planning a mutiny when they were sailing as fellow passengers on the *Susan Constant*. A jury impaneled by Ratcliffe must have believed Smith was innocent of any wrongdoing, because it ruled in his favor.

Soon after Wingfield was removed from office, Ratcliffe, the settlement's new president, named Smith the colony's "cape merchant" or supply officer. In this position, Smith was in charge, he said, "of all things abroad [out of doors]."[8]

By that time, the death toll stood at forty-six, according to Smith. That meant about fifty-five men were still living in squalid conditions within James Towne's fortified palisade. "As yet we had no houses to cover us, our Tents were rotten, and our Cabbins worse than nought . . . ," Smith wrote.[9] If the Indians had mounted an attack at that time they probably would have quickly overrun the weak settlement. Instead, they began trading.

"Our provision being now within twentie dayes spent," Smith said, "the Indians brought us great store both of Corne and bread ready made." At the same time, the James River's surface was suddenly alive with migrating birds, heading south for the winter. The colonists, Smith said, were "greatly refreshed."[10]

Smith soon put the settlers, with food in their bellies, to work strengthening the little town. "By his owne example, good words, and faire promises," one of the settlers later wrote, "he

[Smith] set some to mow, others to binde thatch, some to build houses, others to thatch them; himselfe alwaies bearing the greatest taske for his own share: so that in short time, he provided most of them lodgings, neglecting any for himselfe."[11]

This description of Smith's activities in James Towne—included in the second section of *A Map of Virginia*, published by Smith in 1612—has often been pointed to as a prime example of how ready he was to promote himself. Indeed, while *A Map of Virginia* was published by Smith, its second section is actually a compilation of reports by several of the colonists. If Smith had been more modest, he might have toned down the paragraphs that praised him as a leader. No one, however, ever accused Smith of modesty. At the same time, none of the settlers who were with Smith in Virginia and who returned to England ever claimed his writings were false.

Meanwhile, though the Indians had started limited trade with the James Towne settlers, Smith knew he had to take action to guarantee food for the winter months. He quickly made several voyages to Indian villages to trade trinkets and tools for food.

On one of these voyages, Smith went north to trade with the Chickahominy Indians. This tribe lived on the river of the same name, near the present-day site of Lanexa, Virginia. This voyage was very successful. Smith returned to James Towne with about four hundred baskets filled with corn.

With sufficient grain to feed all the settlers, at least for a time, it seems the conflicts in the settlement might have come to an end. Instead, things got worse. Soon after Smith returned from the journey to the Chickahominies, James Read, James Towne's blacksmith, had an argument with President Ratcliffe. Though it is not clear who started the argument, it seems that the blacksmith either struck or tried to strike the man who was, as president of the colony's ruling council, the embodiment of King James in the New World. After a quick trial, he was sentenced to be hanged.

Settlers traded simple tools, copper bangles, and cheap beads for corn, fish, oysters, venison, and furs.

On the gallows, Read—to save his own life—blurted out the details of a plot hatched by Kendall, apparently with Wingfield's connivance. According to the blacksmith, Kendall planned to steal the pinnace and sail it, with Wingfield and several other companions, across the Atlantic.

In the wake of his confession, Read was pardoned. Kendall was executed, shot to death. Wingfield, probably because of his high status, was not punished at all, though he later admitted he was, indeed, determined to get to England so he could report on the state of the colony, and, no doubt, complain about his treatment at the hands of Smith and the other upstart settlers.

In early December of 1607, following yet another trading voyage up the Chickahominy River, the council ordered Smith to go exploring, to find gold or the river path that led to the Pacific Ocean.

As Smith prepared to leave James Towne, he must have looked forward to escaping once again from the constant bickering within the fort to the relative peace of the wilderness. Little did he know that on this voyage he would find neither the glittering metal that was desired by the Virginia Company nor a path to the wealth of the Orient. Instead, he would find an Indian princess named Pocahontas and an adventure that grew with time to achieve status as an American myth.

CHAPTER EIGHT

The Nonpareil of Virginia

On December 10, 1607, John Smith and a small band of men set out on the voyage of discovery that had been ordered by the members of James Towne's governing council. He was accompanied by Jehu Robinson, one of the settlement's gentlemen; George Cassen, a laborer; Thomas Emry, a carpenter; and six other men.

The waters of the James River were gray, the sky overcast, the north wind cold as Smith and his comrades sailed the colony's shallop northwest up the river to the wide mouth of the Chickahominy. Turning north into the smaller river, the explorers made their way upstream, past the Indian village of Apokant. Pressing on, they rowed and sailed farther north until, late that day, they reached a point where the river narrowed to a shallow, twisting stream. Determined to press on, Smith decided to return to Apokant, where he could leave the shallop under guard and hire a canoe and guides to continue his explorations.

The next day, Smith told six of his companions to remain with the anchored shallop and not to step ashore until his return. He, Robinson, and Emry then set out in a borrowed canoe with two Indian guides.

The canoe carrying Smith and the others glided quickly upriver. The men in the canoe kept paddling until midday when Smith spied a patch of solid ground where the canoe could be pulled ashore. Leaving Robinson and Emry with one of the Indians, he told them to start a fire and prepare a meal while he went exploring on foot with the second guide. Knowing the Indians might attack at any moment, he told his men to keep their muskets near at hand, loaded and ready to fire.

Meanwhile, Smith had barely left Apokant when George Cassen, the laborer, disobeyed Smith's orders and waded from the anchored shallop to the shore, where he was quickly captured by Indians acting on orders of Openchancanough, the great Powhatan's brother. This *werowance*, who hated the Europeans, had gotten word of Smith's foray up the Chickahominy and wanted to know where he was headed, and why.

The Indians, determined to wring information from their captive, quickly tied him to a tree. Cassen, terrified, must have screamed for his friends to come ashore and rescue him. His companions, however, turned tail and fled in the direction of James Towne. Quickly, the Indians hacked their victim's fingers and toes off with mussel shells and dried, razor-sharp reeds. Screaming in terror and agony, Cassen soon told his captors where Smith was bound.

If Cassen thought answering the Indians' questions would end his torture, he was wrong. Having gotten the information they wanted, the Indians started a fire and threw his severed fingers and toes in the flames. They then flayed him alive and gutted him before setting the tree to which he'd been tied ablaze.

Meanwhile, having discovered where Smith was headed, a large group of warriors raced on foot along the river's shore. Before long, they spied Smith's canoe beached and the companions he'd left behind seated around a fire. The Powhatans attacked. In seconds, Jehu Robinson lay dead, struck by twenty or thirty arrows. Thomas Emry and the Indian guide onshore with him were never seen again.

On foot not far from the beach, Smith heard a scream—perhaps Emry's death cry—followed by what he described as "a hollowing of Indians."[1] Though no warning shot had been fired, he knew his men were in trouble. Acting quickly, he grabbed his guide and lashed his left arm to the Indian's right. Holding his cocked pistol to the Indian's head, he warned him that he would shoot if anything had happened to Robinson and Emry.

During the next several minutes, Smith himself came under attack. Using his Indian guide as a shield, he fought a desperate battle for survival. Loading and firing his pistol as fast as he could, Smith managed to keep his attackers at bay. About twenty arrows were shot at him, but they either missed entirely or passed harmlessly through his clothing. His pistol shots, meanwhile, killed two warriors and wounded a third, who later died.

Smith's prowess with his pistol forced a stalemate that continued until some two hundred braves, bows and arrows at the ready, stepped from the woods and edged closer to where he stood with his living shield.

"My hinde [the Indian he had hired]," Smith later said, "treated betwixt them and me of conditions of peace; he [revealed] me to be the Captaine: my request was to retire to the boate."[2]

The fact that Smith was one of the English leaders was probably the only thing that saved his life, for the Powhatan people did not ordinarily execute chiefs or chieftains taken in battle. Still, the Indians were not about to let their valuable captive escape. Telling Smith that the rest of his men had been killed, they demanded that he lay down his arms.

As a soldier, it was Smith's duty not to let his weapons fall into the hands of the Indians if it could be avoided. Still holding his no doubt terrified human shield close, he walked backward, trying to find a way to escape. Paying more attention to the Indians than to his footing, Smith slipped into what he described as an "oasie (oozy) creek."[3]

The Powhatans must have laughed at the sight of Smith foundering in the swamp, sinking deeper and deeper into the freezing mud as he struggled, still holding on to his Indian guide. Finally, "near dead with cold," Smith realized he was beaten.[4] He lay down his weapons and was pulled from the bog.

Under guard, Smith was taken before Openchancanough. Smith had met him when he accompanied Captain Newport on his explorations up the James, and he knew the man to be an important chieftain. Apparently hoping to make Openchancanough believe he was a powerful man, a man with magical powers, Smith pulled an ivory compass from his pocket and gave it to the Indian. "Much they marvailed at the playing of the [compass card] and Needle which they could see so plainely, and yet not touch it, because of the glasse . . . ," Smith later wrote.

Seeing how impressed the Indians were by his "magic," Smith launched into a lecture in which he explained, he later said, "the roundnesse of the earth, and skies, the sphaere of the Sunne, Moone, and Starres, and how the Sunne did chase the night round about the world continually . . . and many other such like matters."

According to Smith, the Indians, who must not have understood a word of his speech, "all stood as amazed with admiration."[5]

If they were, indeed, amazed, their amazement didn't last long for they suddenly grabbed Smith and tied him to a tree. The warriors nearest him nocked arrows and drew their bows.

Openchancanough, however, had other ideas. Perhaps he was acting under orders from Powhatan, or perhaps he found Smith and his compass entertaining. In any case, he moved to stand between Smith and the warriors who were ready to turn him into a human target.

For the next several days, Smith was held captive at Openchancanough's hunting camp, located between the

Chickahominy and Pamunkey rivers. Smith expected to be executed at any moment. Given huge amounts of food to eat, he thought the Indians "woulde fat him to eat him." Not surprisingly, Smith didn't eat much of the food the Indians served him. His stomach, he later confessed, "at that time was not very good."[6]

During this period, the father of the warrior he had wounded just before his capture tried to sneak into the lodge where Smith was being held, hoping to kill him while he slept. Smith's Indian guards, however, managed to stop his attacker.

In the wake of that attack, thinking he might trick the Indians into setting him free, Smith promised his captors he could cure the wounded brave if they allowed him to go to James Towne to get a bottle of special magical water.

The Indians countered with an offer of their own, promising him "life, liberty, land, and women" if he betrayed his comrades and told them how they could safely gain entry to the fort.[7] Smith, of course, said no.

Somehow, he convinced the Powhatans to allow him to send a note to the fort asking for the magic water, some warm clothing, and other supplies. He warned the Indians that his companions would emerge from the fort, ready to fight, as soon as they were spotted, and cautioned them to leave the note where it would be found and to return later to pick up the supplies he requested.

He then tore several pages from a small book he carried and, in his words, "writ his minde to them at the Fort," telling them of his capture and asking for supplies.[8]

It took three days for the messengers to make their way to James Towne and return. Things, they reported, had happened just as Smith had foretold. As they neared the fort, they saw settlers come out, armed and ready to do battle. Cautious, they dropped Smith's note and left. Returning later, they found all the things Smith had asked for.

With no knowledge of written language, the Indians were convinced by this episode that Smith was able to make marks on paper that "spoke" to the settlers in James Towne. They believed he had powerful magic at his control.

Starting sometime around December 18, he was taken, under strong guard, on a "tour" of villages in the Chesapeake region. One of the villages he was taken to was Rappahannock, on the north bank of the river of the same name. This village had been visited a few years earlier by an Englishman—no one knows for sure who—who had killed the village's *werowance*. Now the Indians wanted to see if Smith was the killer.

Luckily for Smith, the Indians at Rappahannock remembered the killer as a tall man. As soon as they saw Smith, they knew he was innocent. (Remarkably, this is the only evidence we have to Smith's short stature.)

Following this tour, Smith was taken to the village of Werewocomoco, the seat of Powhatan's empire, located on the north shore of what is now the York River. When he was led into the village, Smith later reported, "more than two hundred . . . grim Courtiers stood wondering at him, as he had beene a monster."[9]

He was taken into a huge lodge to meet Powhatan himself. The great chief was seated before a roaring fire on a raised platform covered with mats. He was clad in a robe of raccoon skins with their tails still attached. On either side of him sat an Indian girl of about sixteen years of age. These were his favorite wives of the moment—girls who would, according to custom, each bear him a child before being sent away from his presence to marry again. Along each side of the lodge sat two rows of warriors. Behind each man stood a woman.

Soon after Smith entered the lodge, a woman brought him a basin of water to wash his hands. Another brought a bunch of turkey feathers he could use as a towel. Then, platters of food were brought in and placed on the ground.

After feasting on yams and oysters and meat and corn, Powhatan began questioning Smith. For a time, their conversation was friendly. Suddenly, though, the friendly meeting turned unfriendly.

At a command from Powhatan, warriors leapt to Smith's side and held his arms pinned as two great stones were carried into the lodge. Smith was thrown to the ground, and his head was placed on one of the stones. War clubs were raised, ready to beat his brains out.

At that moment, Pocahontas, "the Kings dearest daughter," in Smith's words, "got his head in her arms, and laid her owne upon his to save him from death. . . ." At a signal from Powhatan, the warriors lowered their clubs. John Smith was allowed to live.

This young princess who saved Smith's life was, by all accounts, a remarkable young woman. All who saw her remarked on her beauty. Her portraits—there are several—show her as a striking woman. She was also smart and brave.

Powhatan's daughter, Smith wrote, "much exceedeth" all the other Indians "not only for feature, countenance, and proportion . . . but for wit and spirit." He called her the "Nonpariel" of Virginia, meaning she was without equal.[10] Others who met her shared Smith's opinion.

It is possible, but unlikely, that Smith saw Pocahontas before their famous meeting in Powhatan's longhouse. If he did, he never mentioned it. About twelve years of age when the English arrived in Virginia, she visited James Towne in the company of Indians who came to the fort to trade during the settlement's earliest months.

She made quite an impression on other settlers who saw her at the fort. She would, one of these settlers later wrote, "gett the boyes [cabin boys who came to the colony on the *Susan Constant*] forth with her into the markett place and make them wheele, falling on their hands turning their heeles upwards, whome she would follow, and wheele so her self naked as she was all the fort over. . . ."[11]

While the English settler who wrote about the Indian princess turning naked cartwheels seems to have been shocked by her behavior, it must be noted that for Pocahontas to play this way was not surprising. Powhatan women, both young and

*One of hundreds of images which show Pocahontas saving
the life of John Smith, a dramatic event which has captured the
imagination of people throughout history.*

old, were what one Virginia pioneer described as
"Frolicksom."[12] And the name Pocahontas, given to her by her
family and based on her behavior, means "playful" or "mis-
chievous." (Her real name, the secret or clan name known only
by her family and never spoken in everyday life, was Matoka or
Matoax, meaning "little snow feather.")

If, indeed, Pocahontas had seen Smith in James Towne, she may well have been impressed by his demeanor—or perhaps even his looks—if for no other reason than he was so different from the Indians she knew. In any event, the dramatic scene in which Pocahontas hurls her body on top of Smith's to keep him from being killed by her father's warriors is one of the most famous in American history. However, there have been doubts cast on the truth of this picture. Some scholars have gone so far as to call Smith a liar.

Doubts arise from the fact that Smith never mentioned Pocahontas saving his life in the brief history he wrote of the Virginia Colony in 1608. He didn't tell the whole story until 1624. This fact alone is enough to brand Smith as a liar, at least in some people's eyes.

The truth is that the 1608 history by Smith was a letter that was edited—perhaps heavily edited—before it was published. Who knows what the editor cut out? Also, in 1608 Smith was trying to convince people to come to America as settlers. The story of an Englishman's capture and near-execution by "savages" would hardly have inspired anyone to book passage to the wilderness.

By 1624, the situation had changed. Smith had long been back in England. The Virginia Company was no longer operating. Smith was free to tell the truth—even the embarrassing truth that he, a brave soldier, had been saved by a child, and a girl-child at that!

It must be noted that such rescues were not all that strange among Indian tribes. Eighty years before Smith's rescue, Juan Ortiz, a young member of an expedition in Florida, was captured by Indians near Tampa and saved from being roasted alive by the daughter of an Indian chief.

Scholars now believe that what Smith experienced was a tribal ritual—a ceremony that symbolized the "death" of his old self and rebirth as a new person, an adopted member of the Powhatan people. Of course when Smith's head was placed on the stones before Powhatan he would have fully believed the Indians meant to kill him and that only Pocahontas's actions stopped his execution.

In the final analysis, it seems certain that things happened just as Smith said they did. There is no real reason to doubt the story of John Smith and Pocahontas. There are many reasons to believe it is true.

CHAPTER NINE

Governor of Virginia

The days immediately following his rescue by Pocahontas must have been terrifying for John Smith. Cut off from his friends at James Towne, surrounded by people he considered his enemies, and able to understand only a smattering of their language, he felt certain that he would be put to death at any moment.

His terror must have grown when, not long after his rescue—he was led into an empty longhouse, forced to sit on a mat before a large fire, then left alone. Suddenly, he later wrote, he heard "the dolefullest noyse he ever heard" from behind a hanging mat that divided the longhouse in two. Powhatan, painted so that he looked "more like a devill than a man" appeared from behind the mat with some two hundred warriors all painted black.[1]

Smith's fears, however, were groundless, for Powhatan sat across the fire from him and told him he was to be regarded as his own son. As a token of his friendship, the chief gave the English captain the Indian name Nantaquaus (or Nantaquoud).

Finally, after being in captivity for about three weeks, Smith was freed and sent to James Towne with a dozen Indian guides. For two days, as the party traveled along narrow paths through the forest of winter-barren trees, Smith was constantly on his guard, "still expecting . . . ," he said, "every houre to be put to one death or other."[2]

Though Smith was wary, he had nothing to fear. Not long after sunrise on the second day, he and his companions made their way across the narrow neck of land that joined James Towne and the mainland. As Smith and the others walked out of the woods into the cleared area around the fort, those inside saw them approaching and ran outside to welcome Smith back from his adventure.

Smith must have been overjoyed to be back at James Towne, to find himself surrounded by the familiar sights and sounds and smells of what had become his home. Happy as he must have been, however, he immediately turned his attention to business.

While he had been in Powhatan's custody, the old chief had asked Smith to make a present to him of two of the cannon that guarded the settlement. Willing to agree to almost anything to win his release, he had agreed to the chief's request.

Smith, of course, had no intention of allowing the Indians to carry off two of James Towne's cannon. However, not wanting to openly insult Powhatan, he offered the Indians two "demi-culverins," huge fieldpieces that weighed more than two tons each. With the dry wit he often used when writing about his experiences, Smith later remarked that the Indians found the cannon "somewhat too heavie," to haul back to Powhatan.

Then, to impress his visitors, Smith had the cannon filled with stones and ordered them fired at the trees near the fort. Icicles and branches "came so tumbling downe," he wrote, "that the poor Salvages ran away halfe dead with fear."[3]

After coaxing the Indians back to the fort, Smith gave them gifts of beads and trinkets to carry to Powhatan. He then discovered he had a much more serious matter to tend to.

While Smith was in captivity, President Ratcliffe, probably believing Smith dead, had made Gabriel Archer a member of the settlement's governing council, despite the fact that putting

Archer on the council violated the instructions from the Virginia Company.

Archer, a lawyer and one of Smith's most dedicated enemies, used the Old Testament law to claim that Smith should be hanged because he was somehow responsible for the deaths of Robinson and Emry, the men killed by Openchancanough's warriors. At that time there were some thirty-eight settlers still alive in James Towne. While Smith claimed that most were happy to see him walk from the woods after his release by Powhatan, there were obviously some who would have been happier if he'd been killed. In fact, Archer was quickly able to muster support for his charges against Smith.

Justice was swift in James Towne. According to Edward Maria Wingfield, Smith "had his tryall the same daie of his retorne," and was sentenced to hang almost immediately.[4] It was not yet his time to die, however. Shortly before he was to have been executed, Captain Christopher Newport sailed up the James River to drop anchor just off the fort. John Smith, saved by Pocahontas just a few days earlier, was saved once again, this time on Newport's orders.

On this voyage to the New World, Newport commanded a two-ship fleet. His flagship, the vessel he sailed upriver to James Towne, was the *John and Francis*, which carried about eighty new settlers along with a store of badly needed supplies. A smaller vessel, the *Phoenix*, carrying about forty men and more supplies, had gotten separated from the flagship during the ocean passage and was, when Newport arrived at James Towne, feared lost at sea.

There was no housing for the settlers brought by Newport. Quickly, the healthy newcomers built shelter of some sort for themselves, probably rough-hewn A-frames covered with twigs and dirt or thatch.

The arrival of the newcomers with their supplies must have been heartening to Smith and the other settlers who'd been struggling against overwhelming odds for more than six months. Any joy they felt did not last long, however. Within days of their arrival the fort somehow caught fire. In this fire, a portion of the palisade and all but three of the thatched-roofed wooden buildings inside the fort were destroyed. So were most of the colony's supplies, the settlers' clothing, and their personal belongings.

In the wake of this fire, hunger, sickness, and freezing cold made death a constant visitor at the struggling settlement. However, things could have been much worse. If the fire had started before Newport's arrival, James Towne would almost certainly have been wiped out by hunger, cold, and Indian attacks.

As quickly as they could, the survivors began repairing the damage caused by the fire. In the weeks between mid-January and late February, the sailors and settlers rebuilt the palisade, erected new shelters for themselves, and built at least one storehouse to protect the few supplies that remained. At the same time, they traded with the Indians for food, and buried their dead in the frost-hard ground.

In these weeks, and, indeed, in the months that followed, Pocahontas was a regular visitor to the fort. "Now ever once in foure or five dayes," Smith later wrote, "Pocahontas with her attendants, brought . . . so much provision, that saved many of their lives, that els for all this had starved with hunger. . . . "[5] The maiden who had saved his life—either in reality or as part of a complicated adoption ceremony—obviously felt responsible for his survival and desirous of his well-being.

Newport, at this time, was under pressure from the colony's financial backers either to find a passage to the Pacific Ocean or to discover gold in Virginia. He decided that the great chief Powhatan might be willing to tell his adopted "son" where to find gold or how to proceed to what the English called the Other Sea. In late February, Newport, Smith, and about forty armed men set out to visit Powhatan.

This visit did not go well. Though Powhatan entertained the Englishmen with dancing and feasting and seemed pleased by their gifts of a suit of red cloth, a white greyhound, and a

Pocahontas brings food for the settlers.
The name Pocahontas means "playful one."

stovepipe hat, he revealed nothing about hidden stores of gold
or about a river passage to the Pacific.

Indeed, Newport did more harm than good when he
offered large amounts of copper and even swords in exchange
for corn. Knowing Newport's actions could make English trade
goods nearly worthless, Smith stepped in. Producing a handful
of glass beads "the colour of the skyes," he told Powhatan that
they were rare, so rare that they were worn only by the greatest

kings in the world.[6] As a result of this savvy move on Smith's part, Powhatan was willing to trade some three hundred bushels of corn for just a pound or two of the beads.

In the wake of this journey, Newport turned his full attention to discovering gold. Following his lead, the settlers, Smith said, did nothing but "dig gold, wash gold, refine gold, loade gold."[7] He was being sarcastic. There was no gold in Virginia other than a kind of "fool's gold"—mica, called by Smith "guilded durt."[8]

Their hunger for quick wealth led the settlers to neglect the important work of building permanent dwellings and clearing land for the planting season that was rapidly approaching. Smith was enraged by what he saw as the foolishness of the men sent to the New World by the Virginia Company. The colony, he wrote, would have been better served to have "one hundred good labourers (in place of) a thousand such Gallants as were sent me, that would doe nothing but complaine, curse, and despaire. . . ."[9]

When, in mid-April, Newport finally departed from James Towne, Smith must have breathed a sigh of relief. At last, with Newport and his distractions gone, the settlers might turn their attention to the more important business of surviving in the hostile wilderness.

In fact, with Newport gone, the ninety or so surviving colonists cleared fields and finished repairs on the buildings damaged in the fire. At about the same time, the weather turned warm, a welcome change following the bitterly cold winter.

Then, about ten days after Newport's departure, the *Phoenix*, the ship that had been feared lost at sea, sailed into view. Though it had been forced to take refuge in the West Indies, its captain had carefully conserved the supplies that had been placed in his care, supplies he was now able to deliver to the once-again desperate settlers in the little town.

In early June, the *Phoenix* departed for England with a load of cedar clapboard. The ship also carried a long letter Smith had written to a friend describing the settlement's early days. This letter, edited, later was published as the report we know as *John Smith's True Relation*, famous as the first book ever written in the New World.

Following the departure of the *Phoenix*, Smith set about exploring the James River and its tributaries. For about six weeks, he and a small group of companions explored one river after another. They established contact with a number of Indian tribes, sometimes skirmishing with them, sometimes joining them in what Smith described as "songs and daunces and much mirth."[10]

Smith must have thoroughly enjoyed these dangerous explorations. As uncertain as life was within the palisade at James Towne, he was still drawn to the adventure and excitement he found in the wilds outside the settlement.

In the middle of June, not long after leaving the settlement, Smith and his companions spied a huge school of fish swimming in some shallows near their boat. With cries of delight, the explorers jumped into the shallow water and began spearing fish with their swords. The last fish Smith took was a stingray. As he removed it from his sword, it drove its poisonous barb deep into his wrist. In moments, the poison made his hand and arm swell and throb with pain. Smith—who had narrowly escaped death at the hands of Turkish champions, Indian enemies, and both English and Indian executioners—seemed fated to die as the result of a stingray's attack. In fact, he was so sure he was about to die that he chose a spot on a nearby island where he wished to be buried.

Meanwhile, a surgeon who was included in the exploring party treated Smith the best way he could. Eventually the swelling went down and the pain stopped. Then, in a move typical of the feisty captain, John Smith ate the stingray for his evening meal.

When Smith and the others returned to James Towne in late July, they found virtually all the newcomers—those who had come on the *John and Francis* and the *Phoenix*—sick with

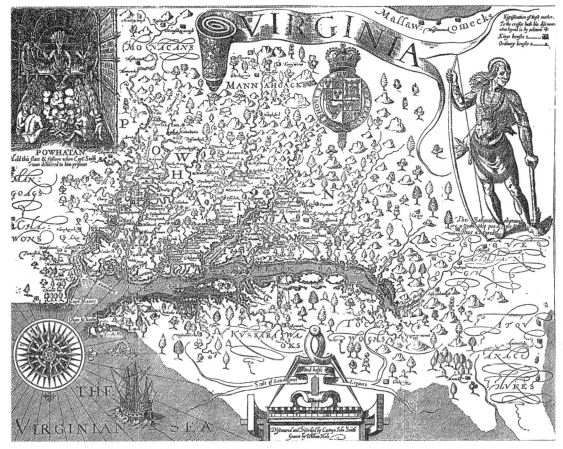

John Smith's map of Virginia territory was still in use in the eighteenth century, when it was used to define the boundaries of the Maryland Colony and to establish the Mason-Dixon line.

the malaria-like illness that laid almost every Englishman low during his first summer in the New World. Miserable, the settlers were blaming their problems on John Ratcliffe, the serving president of the colony.

With Smith back in the fort, the other settlers deposed Ratcliffe from office. They tried to convince Smith to take over as the colony's president or governor. He, however, was more interested in continuing his explorations. He convinced the other settlers to name Matthew Scrivener, a gentleman who had arrived on the *John and Francis*, governor in his place. Then, leaving the men at the fort to "live at ease [and] recover their healths," he set out exploring yet again.[11]

During the next six weeks, Smith and fourteen companions explored the Chesapeake Bay region. They made their way as far north as the head of the bay. From that point they journeyed up the Susquehanna River to a spot close to what is now the border between Pennsylvania and Virginia. Smith mapped the territory through which they traveled, producing a document that was remarkable in its accuracy.

When Smith and his companions returned to James Towne in early September of 1608 they found that Scrivener had, in the brief time he'd been governor, proved to be no more suited to be leader than had Ratcliffe. On September 10, at the request of the majority of the settlers, John Smith was elected governor of James Towne. The yeoman farmer's son, seemingly destined by birth to be a farmer himself and to live his life within a few miles of the place of his birth, was now the governor of England's only colony in the New World.

CHAPTER TEN

The Second Supply

About three weeks after Smith was named governor, an English vessel sailed up the James River to anchor near the fort. This ship, the *Mary and Margaret*, was under the command of Captain Christopher Newport, sent again from England by the colony's financial backers with supplies and additional settlers.

In the fall of 1608 when the ship arrived at the colony, the James Towne settlers were, as they always were in the colony's early days, in desperate need of food. As the ship came to anchor, they must have stood on the slight rise overlooking the water, staring at the vessel with their mouths watering at the thought of filling their growling bellies.

To be sure, the *Mary and Margaret* was heavily laden. It carried presents sent by King James for Powhatan. In addition, the vessel was crowded with about eighty passengers, including about a dozen workmen sent to produce pitch, tar, glass, and ashes used in the making of soap, and some seventy settlers, most of whom were unused to labor. Strapped to the deck was a huge barge, in pieces, for Captain Newport's use as he went exploring. But there was no food for the settlement, not even for the newcomers.

These new recruits increased James Towne's population from about 120 persons to about 200. Among the new settlers were two women—a Mistress Forest, wife of one of the colony's gentlemen, and her maid, Anne Burras. These women were the first women to come to the tiny settlement.

It seems that Mistress Forest did not live long, for other than a brief note about her arrival, her name is not mentioned again in the surviving records of the colony. Anne Burras, however, went on to marry John Laydon, a laborer who was one of the colony's original settlers, soon after her arrival. They would later have a daughter, Virginia, who was the first Anglo-American child born at James Towne.

Remarkably, recent archaeological work done at James Towne uncovered a few bones believed to be those of Mistress Forest. The bones are those of a woman between thirty and forty years of age, about the age Mistress Forest would have been when she arrived in James Towne. Other artifacts found with the skeleton indicate that the burial took place between 1607 and 1610. While it may never be known with certainty whether these bones are actually those of Mistress Forest, Dr. William Kelso, the archaeologist in charge of the James Towne dig, recently wrote "with so few women to choose from, the odds are strong" that the skeleton is hers.[1]

In 1608, John Smith was probably happy to see the two women step ashore; after all, he wanted Virginia to succeed and knew that women would add to the settlement's stability. At the same time, he was enraged when he discovered that the Virginia Company had sent no supplies to speak of. His anger wasn't helped any when he learned that Newport's orders made no mention of providing assistance to the colonists. Instead, the captain was to remain in America until he found gold, a route to the South Sea, or some remnant of the long-lost Roanoke Colony.

As Smith's biographer Bradford Smith speculated, John Smith must have felt like a soldier forced to go into battle without proper weapons, commanded by generals who never visited the front lines and who knew nothing of the terrain or enemy. He knew, as well, that the "generals" who sat warm and comfortable by their fires in London would survive their own mistakes. He and the other settlers, however, might die as a result of the Virginia Company's lack of support. Still, he had no choice but to obey the company's orders and follow Newport's lead.

In fact, with Newport's arrival, Smith's leadership role in the colony was diminished. Two of the new settlers, Captains Richard Waldo and Peter Winne, became members of the governing council and former governor John Ratcliffe—Smith's enemy who had been deposed by the settlers a few months earlier—was restored to the governing body. That meant Smith had virtually no control over the colony's affairs.

Smith must have shook his head in wonder when he learned that Captain Newport planned to stage an elaborate coronation ceremony for Powhatan. This ceremony, ordered by the colony's leaders in London, was to signal to the chief that he was recognized by England as "emperor" of Virginia while, at the same time, signifying Powhatan's acceptance of King James as his ruler.

At first, Newport planned to take 120 men—more than half of James Towne's population—from the fort to Powhatan's village for the ceremony. To Smith, this was completely unacceptable because it would leave the settlement undermanned. Instead, he volunteered to go with just a small group of soldiers to Powhatan's "court" to invite the chief to come to James Towne for the ceremony.

In mid-October, Smith traveled to Werewocomoco with four men. After a voyage overland, then by canoe up the York River, Smith and his companions arrived at the village only to be told by Pocahontas that her father was in another town, about 30 miles (48 kilometers) distant.

That evening, while Smith waited for Powhatan's return, Pocahontas led him to a clearing near the village where she told him to sit on a mat before a fire. Suddenly, he found himself surrounded by a group of about thirty young Indian women, led by Pocahontas. All the women were nearly naked, their skin painted bright colors, wearing deer horns tied to their heads as they danced and cavorted around him in what Smith described as "their infernall passions."[2]

After an hour or so of "this anticke," a great feast was served, with Smith as guest of honor. During this meal, he later reported, the Indian women and girls, including, no doubt, Pocahontas, pressed and crowded around him, crying, "Love you not me? Love you not me?" Finally, the evening's festivities at an end, he was led to a hut by several of these maidens carrying torches to light their way through the thick forest.[3]

Some historians believe the ceremony Smith witnessed was a Powhatan version of the dance of the Corn Maidens, celebrated in October when crops were gathered. If indeed he witnessed a ceremony celebrating the harvesting of the crops, the dance and the "Love you not me?" cries of the maidens were heavy with sexual meaning and invitation.

It should be noted that Pocahontas was about thirteen years of age at this time. She was considered old enough to take a husband, not only by the Indians but also by the English. Indeed, girls of thirteen could legally marry in England as late as the mid-nineteenth century.

It was also true that the Powhatans viewed sexual relations between unmarried men and women as neither sinful nor shameful. This means it would have been natural for Pocahontas or one of the other young Indian women to want to initiate sexual relations with Smith, an adopted member of the tribe, or perhaps to want him as a husband.

There is reason to believe that the relationship between Smith and the Indian princess was innocent. For one thing, no one who was with Smith and Pocahontas in Virginia at that time ever indicated there was anything romantic or sexual about their relationship. For another, there's the matter of the dictionary of the Powhatan language that Smith wrote at about this time. Included in that dictionary is the sentence: *Kekaten pokahontas patiaquagh niugh tanks manotyens neer mowchick rawrenock audowgh*. Smith translates this sentence as "Bid Pokahontas bring hither two little Baskets, and I wil give her white beads to make her a chaine."[4] That sentence is one that a loving older brother or friendly uncle might say to a young girl. And as far as we know, the relationship between Smith and Pocahontas was every bit as innocent.

In any event, Powhatan soon returned to his "court." His response to Smith's invitation to visit James Towne to receive the gifts sent from the king of England would have done credit to any of the great crowned heads of Europe. "If your King has sent me presents," he sniffed, "I also am a king, and this is my land. Your Father (Captain Newport) is to come to me, not I to him. . . ."[5]

Rebuffed by the chief—who was described by one Englishman who met him as having "a forme and ostentacion of such Majestie . . . which oftentimes strykes awe and . . . wonder unto our people"—Smith returned to James Towne.[6] A few days later, the presents sent by King James were dispatched by water while Smith, Newport, and some fifty soldiers traveled overland to the coronation.

At Werewocomoco, the great chief's gifts—a basin and pitcher and a fancy bed with all its furnishings—were set up for Powhatan's inspection. After being convinced that a fine scarlet robe and other fine clothing sent by King James would not harm him, the chief donned his new robes.

As the coronation proceeded, Smith must have had to fight to keep from laughing aloud when Powhatan refused to kneel to receive the crown. Finally, after several of the Englishmen leaned on the chief's shoulders, he stooped just enough for a copper crown to be placed on his head.

At a signal that the coronation had taken place, the English boats on the scene fired a volley of cannon that terrified Powhatan and his people. Assured that no harm would come to

The coronation of Powhatan

them, the chief—perhaps as a sarcastic response to his corona-tion—gave Newport presents of his own: his old, tattered robe and shoes and several bushels of unshucked corn.

In the wake of this ceremony, Powhatan, as Smith had almost certainly warned Newport, became less cooperative. In all probability, he saw through the English attempts to pacify him and knew, more certainly than ever, that the bearded, coat-wearing people fully intended to drive him and his people off their land. His new strategy was to try to starve the English out.

Newport, more interested in finding either gold or the passage to the South Sea than in serving the Virginia settlers, seemed determined to play into Powhatan's hands. In fact, soon after the coronation, he took more than half the settlement's total population on an expedition up the James. Smith, with just eighty men, was left to guard the settlement and to load the *Mary and Margaret* for her return voyage to London.

By taking men away from trade and planting, Newport—certainly not meaning to—guaranteed that the settlement would have no food during the coming winter months. His expedition, meanwhile, proved fruitless. He found no sign of gold and no sign of a water route to the South Sea. Worse, while he promised to return with a large store of corn, he was able to trade for just a few bushels.

While Newport was gone exploring, Smith took the barge up the Chickahominy River in search of food the settlers needed desperately if they were to survive. The Chickahominy Indians, members of the same tribe that had captured Smith almost a year earlier, refused to trade until he threatened force to convince them to load the barge with about one hundred bushels of corn.

Finally, some time in November, the *Mary and Margaret* departed. Thanks largely to Smith's efforts, the ship's hold was filled with clapboard, pitch, tar, and glass that was manufactured in a new factory built a short distance outside the fort.

As the vessel made its way down the James, Smith must have breathed a huge sigh of relief. Newport had been virtually useless to the James Towne settlers. Ratcliffe, a thorn in Smith's side, was a passenger on the ship bound for England—sent home, Smith said, "lest the company [the other settlers] should cut his throat."[7]

All in all, Newport's visit was a disaster. Relations with Powhatan were harmed rather than helped by the absurd coronation ceremony. Instead of leaving the settlement well-stocked with food, Newport had to obtain corn from the settlers to feed his sailors on their return voyage. His futile exploration up the James left many of the settlers who had accompanied him sick and exhausted.

Sometime before Newport departed, John Smith decided to write a letter, his "rude Answer"[8] to a letter that had been sent to him by the officers of the Virginia Company complaining about affairs in the colony. The list of complaints included charges that Smith treated the Indians too harshly, that there was too much squabbling among the settlers, and that the settlement was not realizing profits quickly enough to suit investors.

In his response, Smith made his disgust with Newport and the Virginia Company clear. "Though I be no scholer, I am past a schoole-boy," he said, adding that everything he was reporting about Virginia he "learned . . . by the continuall hazard of [his] life."[9] He then proceeded to list a litany of complaints.

While the voyage of the *Mary and Margaret* had cost the company some two or three thousand pounds, the settlers had not received food or other supplies worth even a hundred pounds, he said.

The barge sent in pieces on the deck of the *Mary and Margaret* was too heavy to be carried above the falls on the James River, even in pieces. "If he [Newport] had burnt her to ashes," Smith wrote, "one [man] might have carried her in a bag; but as she is, five hundred cannot."[10]

The crowning of Powhatan, he predicted, would lead to nothing but trouble for all in the settlement. As for the charge that James Towne was not producing profits, he lay the blame squarely at the feet of the Virginia Company. "When you send againe I intreat you rather send but thirty Carpenters, husbandmen, gardiners, fisher men, blacksmiths, masons, and diggers up of trees, roots, well provided; then a thousand of such [men] as we have," he said.[11]

Then, in a sentence that seems to signify all his frustration, Smith told the stay-at-homes of the Virginia Company exactly why the settlers were hungry and in need of more support from home. "Though there be fish in the Sea, foules in the ayre, and Beasts in the woods, their bounds are so large, they be so wilde, and we so weake and ignorant, we cannot much trouble them," he said.[12]

While this "rude Answer" of Smith's is important because it enables us to see his state of mind when Newport departed from Virginia, he sent several other documents that proved to be of even more historical importance. The first of these was the map he had made earlier of the Chesapeake Bay and the country and rivers around it. The second was a manuscript he called a "Relation of the Countries and Nations" that surround the Chesapeake.

In this document's pages, Smith details Virginia's geography, climate, flora, and fauna, as well as the Indians and their everyday lives, their religious practices, government, and more. As one historian noted, "His devouring eye . . . missed nothing."[13]

This written description and the map are, according to historian Everett Emerson, "the most valuable of Smith's legacies."[14] Smith himself was proud of what he'd accomplished as an explorer and reporter. "I have made as great a discoverie as [Captain Newport], for less charge than he spendeth . . . every meale," he told the Virginia Company.[15]

As proud as he was, though, he had more important matters on his mind after Newport's departure. In early 1609, John Smith turned his attention from exploring to the survival of James Towne.

CHAPTER ELEVEN

Indian Relations

In early 1609, following Newport's departure, James Towne once again faced the threat of extinction. The Indians, of course, were still a danger, but starvation was an enemy more constant even than the Indians, an always-lurking specter that could wipe out the settlement without leaving a trace.

To ensure the survival of the two hundred settlers under his care, Smith had to deal with Powhatan. For his part, the chief had promised to supply the settlement with corn if the English built him a house and provided him with some muskets and swords along with other trade goods. While Smith had no intention of giving Powhatan weapons that his warriors could turn on James Towne, he was willing to trade. Soon after Newport's departure, he sent six men to Werewocomoco to begin building Powhatan's house. Not long after that he departed for the chief's village, accompanied by forty-six volunteers. He and his companions made the journey in the colony's pinnace and one of the small vessels he described as a barge.

The weather was cold as Smith and his men made their way down the James River. Stopping in a friendly village to obtain food, Smith was warned that the great chief planned to kill him. "Captaine Smith," the village chieftain said, "you shall find Powhatan to use you kindly: but trust him not . . . for he hath sent for you onely to cut your throats."[1]

If Smith was worried about Powhatan, he wasn't about to let his fear keep him from visiting the chief. After a delay of about a week, waiting for a winter storm to pass, the party pressed on, arriving at Werewocomoco in mid-January.

Powhatan soon let it be known he would not trade unless the English gave him swords and guns. Smith, onshore with just a handful of his men, understandably refused.

For a time the two leaders haggled, alternating promises of friendship with threats. Smith told the chief he would preserve their friendship unless the Indians forced war by treating the Englishmen badly. Powhatan responded that he wanted to be a friend of the English but warned that he and his people would flee to the north and leave the James Towne settlers to starve if Smith and his men waged war. "Had we intended you any hurt," Smith responded, "long ere this we could have effected it."[2]

As the two men bargained, Smith became convinced that Powhatan was simply waiting for a chance to attack and kill him and his companions. He ordered more of his men ashore. Meanwhile, Powhatan gave word for several hundred of his warriors to prepare to attack. As soon as he was informed that they were in position, he made an excuse to leave Smith alone and fled from the village with his women, children, and most of the supplies Smith wanted. Smith, meanwhile, apparently was unaware that Powhatan's lodge had been surrounded by warriors.

Smith's companions, however, saw what was happening. One of them made his way to Smith and told him of the chief's treachery. Facing overwhelming odds, Smith may well have thought for a moment of his motto, "To Conquer is To Live." Perhaps he remembered, quickly, the lines he had read in the writings of Nicolo Machiavelli a decade earlier when he studied the arts of soldiery in the field not far from his father's farm. "Men and yron finde money and breade . . . ," Machiavelli had written.[3] Now Smith had no choice but to put his "men and yron" to use if he wished to escape a sticky situation and find "breade" to feed those in James Town.

Smith sprang into action. "[W]ith his pilstoll, sword, and target [shield] hee made such a passage among these naked Divels; that at his first shoot, they . . . tumbled one over another, and the rest quickly fled . . . ," he later wrote.[4]

Thanks to his quick action, Smith was able to join his men, who formed ranks and faced the Indians. Seeing the English ready to fight, the warriors changed tactics. All was a misunderstanding, they said. And Powhatan, gone from his village but obviously still nearby, sent Smith a "great bracelet and a chaine of pearle" as a peace offering.[5] Apparently anxious to avoid an open battle with the musket-bearing English, the chief also ordered a small amount of corn to be loaded on the pinnace.

While Smith must have been anxious to be on his way, he and his men were forced to remain in Werewocomoco one more night when the pinnace was left hard aground by the ebbing tide. Powhatan, learning that Smith and his men were still in his village, determined to make another, more underhanded attempt to rid himself of the troublesome, bearded Englishman.

That night Pocahontas, who must have accompanied her father as he fled from his village, sneaked back through what Smith described as the "darke night" and "irksome woods" to warn Smith that her father planned to slaughter him and his men as they slept.[6] Her warning put Smith on guard. All that night, he and his companions sat with their muskets at the ready, until the tide rose enough to float the barge and pinnace.

Thankful for Pocahontas's warning, John Smith tried to give her gifts. "But," he later wrote, "with teares running downe her cheekes, shee said shee durst not be seene to have any: for if Powhatan should know [she had warned the English], she were but dead."[7]

In the wake of this attempt to kill the invaders, Powhatan decided he had nothing to gain in attempting to bargain with Smith and the other coat-wearing people. Leaving his village, he retired to a hideaway far north of James Towne. From there, he continued overseeing sporadic attempts to drive the English from his lands. But he and Smith were never to meet again. Nor was John Smith to see Pocahontas again for many years.

Meanwhile, having escaped Powhatan's traps, but still without a sufficient supply of desperately needed corn, Smith left Werewocomoco and led his men up the Pamunkey River to the village of Openchancanough, the great chief's brother. Openchancanough, who would ultimately prove to be a much greater enemy to the English than Powhatan, followed his brother's lead and pretended a willingness to trade even as he plotted Smith's murder.

As the chief and Smith negotiated, Openchancanough moved some seven hundred warriors into position around his village, ready to attack. Warned of their presence, Smith urged the handful of men in his party to stand fast. "God will so assist us," he said, "that if you dare stand but to discharge your pieces, the very smoake will bee sufficient to affright them. . . . [L]et us fight like men, and not die like sheepe. . . ."[8]

In the midst of this drama, Smith managed to grab Openchancanough by his hair and hold a cocked pistol to his chest. He reminded the Indians that they had granted him mercy when he was trapped in the mire of the swamp. He said their former kindness almost convinced him that they still meant him no harm. "But if I be the marke you ayme at, here I stand, shoot he that dare," he said. Then he made a threat they could easily understand. "You promised to [load] my Ship ere I departed," he told the Indians, "and so you shall; or I mean to load her with your dead carcasses. . . ."[9]

The Indians quickly complied.

Captain Smith survived an ambush by trapping chief Openchancanough and threatening to kill him, although the Indians continued to make attacks against the settlers.

At the same time, a great deal was happening both at Werewocomoco and at James Towne.

In the Indian village, several of the laborers Smith had dispatched to build Powhatan's dwelling turned traitor after they were convinced by the Indians that it was better to serve the great chief than to starve to death in James Towne. With the help of these traitors—and the gullibility of the men Smith had left in charge at the settlement—Powhatan was able to obtain three hundred hatchets, fifty swords, eight muskets, and an equal number of pikes.

At about the same time, tragedy struck the settlement. Matthew Scrivener, the man Smith had left in charge, set out on a hunting expedition in a small skiff. Accompanying him on this hunting party were ten other men, including Captain Richard Waldo, one of the new members of the ruling council, and Anthony Gosnold, the brother of Captain Bartholomew Gosnold who died during the settlement's earliest days. As the eleven settlers set out (against Smith's orders that all should remain at the fort) a winter storm was roiling the James River. Their overloaded little skiff capsized somewhere between James Towne and a nearby island. All the men on board were drowned.

When Smith learned of this tragedy and of the loss of weapons to Powhatan, he determined to return to James Towne, stopping briefly at Werewocomoco to trade for additional corn and to try to punish the traitorous laborers. He and his companions were too late, however. They found Powhatan and his supplies gone and the village virtually empty.

At the end of this trouble-filled expedition, Smith and his men carried almost five hundred bushels of corn and two hundred pounds of deer fat to James Towne. At the same time, the men on the expedition—about 25 percent of the colony's total population—had been fed at the expense of the Indians for a period of six weeks, no mean feat in itself. The total cost to the colony for all this fresh food was just twenty-five pounds of copper and about fifty pounds of iron and beads.

Smith, writing after the fact, put the importance of this accomplishment in perspective. "Men may thinke it strange," he said, "there should be such a stirre for a little corne, but had it been gold with more ease wee might have got it." Without the food, he added, "the whole Colony [would have] starved."[10]

On this trading voyage we see John Smith both at his best and at his worst. We see the bold soldier, quick to take action and brave in the face of danger. We see a man willing to do whatever is required to protect and preserve the colony he served. We also see a suspicious man (though his suspicions were often justified). We see a man who acts rashly, on occasion, and a man who is willing to treat the Indians harshly when he feels it necessary.

Indeed, the officers of the Virginia Company (and some historians since Smith's time) have faulted Smith's "get tough" policy with the Indians. And there is no denying that he could be tough when toughness was required.

In judging John Smith and his actions, it must be remembered that he was first and foremost a soldier. He was the governor of a tiny colony with a population of some two hundred men and two women. This handful of Englishmen and women were surrounded by as many as nine thousand Indians who wanted to drive the English from Virginia. At the same time, Smith had to rely on these Indians to supply him with the food he needed to keep his colony from starvation. Toughness was his only recourse.

It can't be denied that Smith and the other English were wrong in simply coming to America and stealing Indian lands. However, it is a mistake not to place John Smith and his actions in historical perspective. The typical English settlement builder in the New World of America saw nothing wrong with expanding England's holdings by taking land that was, they believed, being wasted by people they considered "savages." It should also be remembered that—as wrong as it is to us—Smith and most of the other settlers believed they were on a holy mission to civilize and Christianize the Indians.

Historian J. A. Leo Lemay called Smith "the Indians' best friend" during the entire colonial period in Virginia. "Within the early seventeenth-century context," he added, "Smith's behavior was not only fair, he was surprisingly kind and humanitarian. He treated Indians as he treated whites."[11]

At the same time, Smith knew that the Indians and the English in Virginia were locked in a war for control of the land. The Indians wanted to see the intruders dead or, at the very least, driven from the land. Smith was equally determined to establish a settlement. If necessary to guarantee his own survival, he would kill the Indians (or any enemy) in battle. If necessary to guarantee food for James Towne, he would threaten, cajole, and, on occasion, even burn Indian longhouses.

If Smith felt any sense of satisfaction about gathering food supplies in late 1608 and early 1609 it was short-lived. For in what must have seemed the blinking of an eye, James Towne would once again be faced with the specter of extinction. And once again John Smith's resourcefulness would be stretched to the limit to keep the English settlement from disaster.

CHAPTER TWELVE

Times of Trial

It is easy to imagine Smith in the days following his return to James Towne from his adventure-filled trading voyage. It is easy to picture him climbing to one of the fort's gun platforms to look over the cluster of crude huts that served as homes for the people who were trying to establish a settlement in the wilds of the Virginia frontier. It is easy, as well, to imagine him feeling helpless and hopeless as he surveyed the tiny settlement.

For almost two years, the English had been in Virginia. What did they have to show for their trials? What had they gained in exchange for the lives of the scores of men who had been killed by hunger, disease, Indians, and by the unforgiving country itself? It would have been natural for Smith to ask himself those questions, especially in the wake of the deaths of Matthew Scrivener, Richard Waldo, and the others who'd drowned in the James. It would also have been natural for him to wonder what he could possibly do to help this tiny toehold of English civilization survive.

His answer was to impose discipline—military discipline—where there had been none. And, since Peter Winne—the sole surviving member of the governing council after Scrivener and Waldo died—himself died of illness early in 1609, Smith had a free hand to impose this discipline as he saw fit.

One of the first things he did was end what he saw as the laziness of some of the settlers, especially the highborn who were not used to physical labor, and who expected others to provide them with food.

"You see now that power resteth wholly in my selfe," he told the settlers not long after his return from Werewocomoco. "You must obey this now for a Law, that he that will not worke shall not eate (except by sicknesse he be disabled:) for the labours of thirtie or fortie honest and industrious men shall not be consumed to maintaine an hundred and fiftie idle loyterers."[1]

With this policy in place, the situation in James Towne rapidly improved. The colonists began producing moneymaking commodities including tar, pitch, and glass at the "glass house" a short distance from the fort. Twenty new houses were built within the palisade and about forty acres of land were cleared and planted. A well—the first well in the settlement—was dug. At the same time, a blockhouse was built near the neck of land that joined what is now Jamestown Island to the mainland. Armed men at this blockhouse were able to control the movement of Indians to and from the fort.

In addition, Smith sent men to build an earthwork "fort" on a rise across the James River from the settlement. This easily defensible position was designed to serve as a retreat in case the main settlement came under attack either by the Indians or the Spanish.

In April 1609, even as the settlement appeared to be achieving stability, the ugly threat of famine once again loomed when it was discovered that corn that was to have sustained the settlement until the harvest was ready to be reaped was half rotten. Rats that had come ashore from the ships were rapidly eating the grain that was not rotten. "This did drive us all to our wits end," Smith later wrote, "for there was [no food] in the country but what nature afforded."[2]

While a few friendly Indians brought turkey, squirrel, and deer meat to the fort, these gifts of food were not enough to

Colonists in Jamestown work together to build new houses.

keep starvation at bay. Smith sent about eighty men down the river to live on oysters, while twenty went with George Percy to Point Comfort—the spot where the settlers had first landed—to try to survive on fish.

Under Smith's leadership, the colony managed to survive; though some of the settlers still at the fort refused to gather food even to feed themselves. In Smith's words, these "distracted Gluttonous Loyterers" would all "have starved or have eaten one another" had he not forced them to gather whatever food could be found.[3] Soon many of these settlers, disgusted by the hunger and squalor that was their constant lot in James Towne, let it be known they wanted to flee the colony.

On July 10, in the midst of all this turmoil, a vessel named the *Mary and John* sailed up to Jamestown and dropped anchor. This ship, under the command of Captain Samuel Argall, was a fishing vessel, sent by the Virginia Company in search of a salable cargo. She did have some desperately needed food and wine on board. "Though it was not sent us, our necessities was such as inforced us to take it," Smith said in his straightforward fashion.[4]

The ship also brought news that the Virginia Company was sending a large fleet of ships and several hundred new settlers to the colony.

A month after the arrival of Argall's ship, the first four ships of this great fleet sailed into the Chesapeake to drop anchor off James Towne. Smith must have been bewildered and angry when the passengers trooped ashore led by none other than John Ratcliffe, Gabriel Archer, and John Martin—three of the original council members who had caused him and the colony nothing but trouble before they had fled or been sent back to England.

His anger only grew when he learned that a total of nine ships had been sent from England carrying not only six hundred settlers and supplies but also a new charter, and new leaders. These new leaders included Sir Thomas Gates, named by the Virginia Company to serve as governor; and Sir George Somers, named Admiral of Virginia. According to the new charter, Smith was removed from office and given a minor job in the government.

Smith's disgust with this turn of events was plain in what he later wrote. The men, including himself, who were responsible for the survival of the little colony had been replaced, he said, without any regard for their accomplishments or feelings. It was, he added, "his ill chance to end, when he had but onely learned how to begin."[5]

If John Smith had been lucky, he would have been removed from office with the coming of the first ships of what has come to be called the Third Supply. Instead, events transpired that were to force him to remain Virginia's governor until the end of his one-year term. As a result, his time in Virginia was to come to a sad and bitter end.

Unknown to any in James Towne, all the new leaders of the colony had sailed on the same vessel, the *Sea Venture*. This ship also carried the commissions of the new colonial leaders, a copy of the charter, instructions for the new leaders, and most of the supplies meant to sustain the hundreds of new settlers.

If this vessel had made it to James Towne in the summer of 1609, Smith would have had the option of giving up his post with some dignity and honor. As it was, he had no legal authority to give up his own commission, even though his old enemies Ratcliffe and Archer demanded that he remove himself from office.

In fact, the *Sea Venture* had been blown far off course by a hurricane and had run aground on coral rocks just off the coast of Bermuda. As fate would have it, the ship drove bow first between two rocks and got stuck there. Though it would never sail again, it was high enough out of the water for all of the 150 passengers, the crew, and the ship's dog to make it to land.

Once ashore, the crew used lumber and rigging from the wrecked *Sea Venture* to build two new vessels they named *Deliverance* and *Patience*. Eventually (though it would take them almost a full year), these survivors would make their way to James Towne. In mid-1609, however, when Smith and the others were waiting for the vessel to appear with its important passengers and the documents that would have relieved Smith of his duties, no one had any idea what had become of it.

Meanwhile, as the survivors of the *Sea Venture* wreck set about rescuing themselves, the balance of the Virginia fleet straggled into James Towne. The settlers brought by this fleet were an unruly group. "(T)hose lewd Captaines [Ratcliffe &c.] led this lewd company, wherein were many unruly Gallants packed thither by their friends to escape ill destinies," Smith later reported, adding that the newcomers tried to overthrow

The Sea Venture *shipwrecked in Bermuda. One of the passengers, William Strachey, kept a journal about the shipwreck and the survival of the castaways. William Shakespeare eventually read this account and used it as the basis for his play,* The Tempest.

the government. "Happie had we beene had they never arrived . . . ," he continued, "never was more confusion, or misery, then their factions occasioned."

Still the man of action, Smith "layd by the heels" the main troublemakers.[6] In modern language, that means he put Archer and Ratcliffe, and perhaps some others in jail, probably in a belowground dungeon that had been constructed not long before the arrival of the newcomers.

In the midst of all these troubles with the newcomers, Smith determined to establish a second trading post and fort. To accomplish that end, he sent one of the new arrivals, a gentleman named Francis West, up the James with about 120 men. West—the brother of Lord De la Warre, who had been placed in overall control of the colony but who had not yet set sail from England—chose a spot near what is now Richmond, Virginia's capital. No sooner had he departed from James Towne, however, he began plotting to force Smith from office.

Meanwhile, as September neared, Smith—by that time heartily sick of trying to govern the colony—tried to convince Martin to take his place. But Martin knew his own limitations. Within hours, he resigned from office, throwing the mantle of authority back on John Smith's shoulders.

Once again in office, Smith soon had to travel up the James to deal with West and his men who refused to work, stole corn from the Indians, and terrorized them.

After several days at West's Fort, Smith grew disgusted with the quarrelsome, troublemaking, often lazy settlers. He set out with a few of his trusted followers, sailing down the James to the settlement that had been his home for almost three years.

No one knows for sure what happened on this return voyage except that Smith fell asleep in his canoe and that someone, somehow, accidentally or on purpose, ignited the bag of gunpowder he carried on his belt.

Screaming, Smith wakened. The burning gunpowder, he said, "tore the flesh from his body and thighes, nine or ten inches square in a most pittifull manner. . . . (T)o quench the tormenting fire, frying him in his cloaths he leaped over-board into the deepe river, where ere they could recover him he was neere drowned."[7] By the time he arrived in James Towne, almost one hundred miles to the south, he was near death.

Smith must have suffered terribly. There was little that could be done to make him comfortable or to heal his ghastly wound. But even as he lay in bed in pain, his enemies plotted his murder. According to Smith, the plan failed when his assassin's "heart did faile" before he was able to "fire that mercilesse Pistoll."[8]

After this attempt on his life, John Smith finally knew he was beaten. He knew he had no choice but to leave the land he had grown to love. Though he tried to leave on a ship that was scheduled to sail the very next day, Ratcliffe and Martin and his other enemies managed to delay the vessel's sailing for three weeks. During that time, documents listing a variety of complaints against Smith were drawn up for delivery to the Virginia Company.

Finally, on October 4, the ship carrying John Smith back to England dropped down the James, bound for the open ocean and London.

Smith could not have known as he sailed away from James Towne that he was never to see Virginia again.

CHAPTER THIRTEEN

In England Again

It was December of 1609 when John Smith returned to London. Though he had already experienced enough adventures to fill the lives of several men, he was still not yet thirty years of age.

Unfortunately, Smith did not leave any record of what he did upon his return to England. We can be sure, however, that he took time to recuperate from the injury he suffered when his powder bag exploded and to regain his strength after his three years of hunger and privation in Virginia.

Soon after his return, Smith turned his attention to the serious business of defending himself against criticisms leveled against him by his enemies in James Towne. To answer these charges, Smith almost certainly met with officials of the Virginia Company. While no record remains of what he said in his own defense, we can be sure he argued vehemently against the reports that had been sent to London by John Ratcliffe, George Percy, and others who had found him overbearing.

At the same time, he began overseeing the publication of a history of the Virginia adventure. This narrative, *The Proceedings of the English Colonie in Virginia*, was published in 1612 at least in part to answer charges that he had treated the Indians harshly and that it was his fault the colony did not produce profits for its investors. While he is often named as the author of this book, it was, in fact, a collection of accounts written by other Virginia settlers and edited by Smith.

Meanwhile, the best evidence in Smith's favor was what happened in Virginia after his return to England. There, in short order, Ratcliffe and some fifty men traveled on a trading voyage to the Pamunkey River. Through what Percy described as a "want of circumspection," Ratcliffe managed to quickly anger Powhatan, who turned on the colonists and killed almost all in the party.[1] Ratcliffe, a harsh critic of Smith's treatment of the Powhatan people, was tied naked to a tree by the Indians and flayed alive. Of fifty men who went up the Pamunkey, only sixteen made it back to the settlement.

At about the same time, Francis West, the settler who had caused Smith so much trouble at the falls not far from present-day Richmond, gathered a group of malcontents, stole a ship, and sailed from the settlement back to England.

As bad as these events were, they hardly gave a hint of what was to happen. With Smith gone, trade between the English and the Indians almost ceased. Starvation soon swept the colony and scores of settlers died. According to George Percy, the situation became so desperate that the colony's dogs were eaten. When they were gone, some of those who died from hunger were dug from their graves and devoured. One man was executed after it was discovered that he had killed his wife, salted her dismembered body, and eaten her.

In writing about this horrible incident, Smith employed a soldier's gallows humor, perhaps as a way to lessen his revulsion. "Now whether shee was better roasted, boyled or carbonado'd [grilled], I know not, but of such a dish as [salted] wife I never heard of," he said.[2]

When Smith learned what had transpired in James Towne during what has come to be known as the Starving Time, he must have pointed with horrified pride to his own record as governor. As filled with strife as James Towne had been while he was its leader, fewer than twenty settlers of the two hundred under his command had died while he was governor. And eleven of those were the men who drowned in the James River when they disobeyed his orders and left the fort.

With Smith gone, the death toll was terrible. Of some five hundred men, women, and children in the colony when Smith departed in the fall of 1609, only about sixty were alive just six months later.

At least some of the colonists left in James Towne must have wondered, then, why they had driven the feisty captain back to England. One of those settlers put his feelings into words that were included in the book Smith published in 1612.

"Thus we lost him . . . whose adventures were our lives, and whose losse our deathes," he wrote.[3]

In late May of 1610, just as the little colony appeared destined for extinction, two small pinnaces appeared in the Chesapeake. They were the *Deliverance* and the *Patience*. On board were about 140 survivors of the *Sea Venture* shipwreck in Bermuda who had built the two vessels to carry them to what they thought would be a thriving settlement.

These survivors were shocked as they looked around James Towne and saw only squalor and starvation. "We found the Pallisadoes torne down . . . , the Gates from off the hinges, and emptie houses . . . rent up and burnt, rather than the dwellers would step into the Woods . . . to fetch other firewood," one of the newcomers said. The settlers themselves, he added, were "so Leane thatt they Looked lyke [skeletons] Cryeinge owtt we are starved."[4]

Among the *Sea Venture* survivors who arrived in James Towne in 1610 were Sir Thomas Gates and Sir George Somers, highborn men who had been named leaders of the colony before their departure from England. Seeing the state of the settlement when they arrived, these two men almost immediately gathered the sixty or so settlers still alive, loaded them on a ship and set sail for England. Remarkably, as they sailed down the Chesapeake they met a boat carrying a message that Lord De la Warre had arrived with a new group of settlers and supplies for all. If Lord De la Warre had not shown up when he did, James Towne would have been abandoned.

While Smith might have thought the terrible news from Virginia would rehabilitate his reputation in England, it had little effect. Ultimately, while he was never found responsible for any wrongdoing in James Towne, neither did he ever receive a public vote of confidence from the Virginia Company.

It is likely that Smith did not help his own cause when it came to pleading his case with the Virginia officials in England. Never afraid to speak his mind in his written reports to the Virginia Company, he would not have minced any words when telling the armchair warriors in London about their mistakes in establishing the colony. For obvious reasons, they were not about to put him—an upstart commoner—in charge of any colonial ventures.

In the years following his return to England, Smith chafed at his inability to return to the New World. He knew that Virginia was a place of vast opportunity both for England and for himself. Always desirous of being in the middle of the action, he must have been like a caged animal, searching for a way to escape civilization and to return to the dangerous wilderness that was his element.

During those years, interest was increasing in the settlement of the lands then known as Northern Virginia, between the Chesapeake Bay and New France (Canada). For many years, this territory had been regularly visited by fishing and trading vessels from England, France, and Holland. No serious effort, however, was made to establish a colony there until 1607, when a group of merchants in Plymouth tried unsuccessfully to found a settlement in what is now Maine.

In April 1614, Smith, with backing of those same merchants—known as the Plymouth Company—was placed in command of two small ships bound for the coast of Northern Virginia. His orders were to "take Whales and . . . make tryalls of a Mine of gold. . . ."[5]

While it turned out that the fleet was unable to take whales, and that there was no gold to be found, there were fish to be caught. Smith left most of his men pulling cod from the waters off the coast of New Hampshire while he and about eight companions went exploring. As he had done in the Chesapeake region, Smith put his abilities as a mapmaker to good use on this voyage of exploration.

"I have drawne a Map from Point to Point, Ile to Ile, and Harbour to Harbour, with the Soundings, Sands, Rocks, and Land-markes as I passed close aboord the shore in a little Boat," he later wrote.[6]

Smith did more than draw a definitive map of the coastline from Cape Cod to a point near Frenchman's Bay in Maine. He also gave the region he explored the name "New England." His map was printed in *A Description of New England* in 1616.

In many people's minds, John Smith's story begins and ends with his time in Virginia. Even historians often overlook his links to New England. Yet, as one historian noted, "whatever else [John Smith] might have achieved . . . , his exploration of New England would alone have earned his right to future fame."[7] And Samuel Eliot Morison, perhaps the greatest of all New England historians, pointed to Smith as one of the region's greatest pioneers. "Few of her founders gave so much," he noted, "and got so little as Captain John Smith."[8]

The time John Smith spent in New England only heightened his desire to lead a settlement in the New World. He loved New England every bit as much as he loved Virginia. He saw, before any other English explorer or colonist, great opportunities where others saw only inhospitable lands and harsh weather.

In the final analysis, Smith's first voyage to New England was a success. He brought back not only his famous map but also about 50,000 pounds of fish and some valuable furs. In recognition of this accomplishment, the Plymouth Company honored him with the title Admiral of New England.

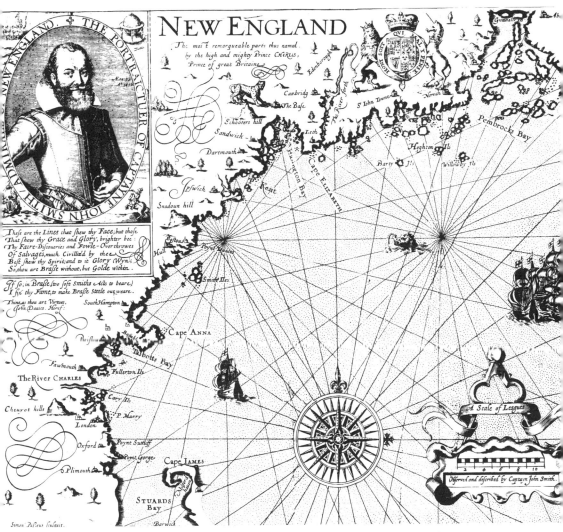

Smith's map of New England was used by many explorers
and settlers who came later, including the Pilgrims who settled
Plymouth Colony in 1620.

With his new title, Smith was able to look forward to more voyages to the New World and, perhaps, some financial rewards. Indeed, he started making plans to send another expedition to New England the following year. These plans fell through, however. Several other planned ventures also came to nothing when financial backers refused to put their money at risk without some hope of finding gold or when ships bound for the New World were turned back by storms.

In May 1616, as Smith devoted almost all his energies to finding some way to return to the New World, a good friend from that distant world reentered Smith's life when Pocahontas came to England.

Captured by the English after Smith's return to England, and held hostage to guarantee peace between the settlers and Powhatan, Pocahontas had, after several years, converted to Christianity. She adopted European ways, and took the name Rebecca. Eventually, she met and married John Rolfe, a settler who gained fame for introducing West Indian tobacco to Virginia and growing it as a very profitable cash crop. Now, in early 1616, she was in England with Rolfe and their infant child, Thomas.

As soon as Smith learned of Pocahontas's arrival in England, he wrote a long letter to Queen Anne, wife of King James I. In that letter, he told how the Indian princess had saved his life in Virginia. He also recounted her long service to the settlers in James Towne.

Remarkably, Smith was in no hurry to visit the woman who had stopped his execution in Powhatan's longhouse almost a decade earlier. Perhaps he was ashamed that he had left Virginia without saying farewell, though she would surely have understood once she knew how badly he had been wounded before his departure. Or perhaps the proud captain who had been the leader in Virginia was ashamed to have the woman now called Lady Rebecca Rolfe see him in his diminished state in England. In any event, Smith did not visit her until late

Ætatis suæ 21. Aᵒ.1616.

In 1614, Pocahontas married John Rolfe, an English settler in the colonies, possibly to help make peace between the settlers and the Indians. Not only did she adopt the English style of dress but she took the English name Rebecca as well.

1616, when she was living with her husband and child in Brantford, a borrowed estate near London.

Unfortunately, Smith only wrote a few lines about this visit. Even these few lines, though, paint a picture of an emotional, almost heartbreaking meeting.

When Pocahontas first saw him, Smith later wrote, the princess turned away and would not speak to him.

What did Pocahontas feel when she saw Smith standing in the parlor of her borrowed mansion? She obviously felt angry and sad that he had not visited her in the eight months she had been in his country. But it was anger mixed with love and, no doubt, regret that she and Smith had been cruelly separated by events in far-off Virginia. For a time, after all, the bearded Englishman and she had been as close as father and daughter.

Pocahontas's feelings were complicated by the fact that after Smith's departure, she had been told by the English in Virginia that he was dead. Indeed, she had not learned he was alive until her arrival in England. Now, suddenly, the man she had so long thought was dead was standing before her—older, probably a little heavier, than when she had last seen him, probably a little down at the heels, but alive and once again in her presence. When she turned away it was almost certainly because she was weeping. In any event, she was so disturbed that John Rolfe took Smith and some companions who had accompanied him aside to give her a chance to regain her composure.

It was several hours before Pocahontas rejoined Smith and the others. She immediately criticized him for neglecting her. She reminded him that when he was a stranger in Virginia he had called Powhatan "father." She then addressed him the same way.

Smith, mindful of her rank as the daughter of a king, told her it was wrong of her to call him by that title. She responded like the princess she was. "Were you not (brave enough) to come into my fathers Country, and caused feare in him and all his people (but mee), and feare you here I should call you father," she said. "I tell you then I will (call you father), and you shall call mee childe, and so I will bee for ever and ever your Countrieman," she said.

And then, in a note of unmistakable pain, she cried, "They did tell us alwaies you were dead, and I knew no other till I came to Plimouth. . . ."9

All that Pocahontas said on this visit showed how she cherished John Smith. Some writers have used her words to make a case that Smith and the Indian princess were lovers in Virginia and that Pocahontas loved him even after her marriage to John Rolfe. In fact, her words and actions can just as easily be interpreted as perfectly innocent. When Pocahontas called Smith "father" in 1616 she was speaking as innocently as Smith himself was almost a decade earlier when he wrote of her in his dictionary of the Powhatan language.

Of course, we will never be able to clearly define the nature of their relationship. What we do know is that Smith was, for a short time at least, a frequent visitor at the estate where Pocahontas lived in England. He must have been proud when she was finally invited to meet the king and queen at court in London. The Indian princess favorably impressed the highborn gentlemen and ladies at the court.

Sadly, even as Pocahontas was honored at Whitehall Palace, her story was nearing its end. In March, as she and her son and husband sailed down the River Thames on their way back to Virginia, she fell sick. The vessel put in at Gravesend, a Thames River port about halfway between London and the open ocean. Within just a few days she was dead, probably a victim of tuberculosis.

The death of the Indian princess was followed about a year later by the death of her father, Powhatan. When Smith heard the news of the old chief's death in mid-1618, coming so soon after the death of his daughter, it would have been perfectly natural for him to take stock of his own life.

Almost forty years of age, he must have been tired. Though still young by our reckoning, he had lived a trying life, filled with battles and hardships. He almost certainly suffered from

Pocahontas with her son by John Rolfe, Thomas. Thomas went to school in England, but later joined the colonists in Virginia.

malaria or other chronic health problems as a result of his time in Virginia.

The thought of turning his back on adventuring once and for all must have entered his mind. Still, he tried one more time to make his way to the New World. In 1619, he offered to serve as military leader for the group of religious dissidents we know as the Pilgrims. At that time these founders of Plymouth Colony were making plans to establish their settlement. Though Smith would have made an excellent general, he was turned down by the Pilgrims, who hired an experienced mercenary soldier named Myles Standish.

By this time, John Smith was desperate to find a way to make his way to New England. How difficult it must have been for him—the man of action, the knight-errant who saw the uninhabited vastness of the New World as his ultimate challenge—to realize that his life of adventuring was at an end.

Yet John Smith was not ready to stop striving to make the territories he loved across the great Atlantic Ocean a fruitful part of the English empire. His work would just have to take a different form.

Adventure's End

In the years between 1620 and 1630, John Smith made only a few halfhearted attempts to return to the New World. Instead, he spent most of his time writing books praising America and promoting it as a land of opportunity. One of his most famous books, *The Generall Historie of Virginia, New England, and the Summer Isles*, was written at this time.

In March of 1622, the Indians of Virginia, led by Openchancanough, Powhatan's brother, rose to drive the English "invaders" into the sea. In a series of swift and unexpected attacks, about 350 colonists were killed.

John Smith's immediate response was to write to the Virginia Company, offering to lead one hundred soldiers and thirty sailors to Virginia either to drive the Indians from their lands or to force them into subjection. Once again, however, Smith was disappointed in his effort to get a commission that would take him back to the New World.

Told he would not be sent to Virginia, Smith began writing the history of the earliest English settlements in Virginia, New England, and Bermuda. The end result, published in 1624, was a book that has been ranked among the most important early American histories. In fact, one historian called Smith "the father of Anglo-American history."[1]

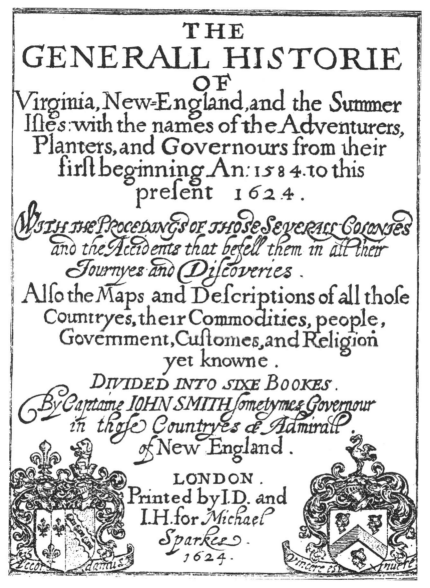

THE GENERALL HISTORIE
OF
Virginia, New=England, and the Summer Isles: with the names of the Adventurers, Planters, and Governours from their first beginning An: 1584. to this present 1624.

WITH THE PROCEDINGS OF THOSE SEVERALL COLONIES and the Accidents that befell them in all their Journyes and Discoveries.

Also the Maps and Descriptions of all those Countryes, their Commodities, people, Government, Customes, and Religion yet knowne.

DIVIDED INTO SIXE BOOKES.

By Captaine IOHN SMITH sometymes Governour in those Countryes & Admirall of New England.

LONDON.
Printed by I.D. and I.H. for Michael Sparkes.
1624.

Title page of Smith's Generall Historie of Virginia. *Smith wrote this account of life in Jamestown, Virginia, and New England to help promote colonization and to guarantee that the early history of the colonies would not be lost.*

About two years later, Smith wrote a book of advice for sailors, a volume popularly known as *A Sea Grammar*. In fact, it was the first manual for seamen written in the history of England. It included a glossary of nautical terms, a section on waging war at sea, and an explanation of the duties of every ship's officer, along with other advice for those he called "learners" and "Saylers."

He followed that book with a volume that told his own life story: *The True Travels, Adventures, and Observations of Captaine John Smith, in Europe, Asia, Affrica, and America.*

In late 1630, at the age of forty-nine, Smith wrote a book of advice for would-be settlers, *Advertisements for the Unexperienced Planters of New England*. This book, Smith's last, was published the following year.

While John Smith, in these years, found a slight measure of success and recognition, he was more than a little bitter about the turns his life had taken. Reduced to near poverty, he complained that he had earned virtually nothing from all his toils in the New World.

Indeed, Thomas Fuller, a contemporary of Smith's, said that Smith "led his old age in London, where (he had) a prince's mind imprisoned in a poor man's purse. . . . " His days must have been filled, as Fuller said, "with the remembrance and relation of what formerly he had been, and what he had done."[2]

And yet, as disappointed as he was by his lack of recognition and financial security, Smith still loved Virginia and New England.

"By that acquaintance I have with them, I may call them my children;" he wrote, "for they have been my wife, my hawks, my hounds, my cards, my dice, and in total my best content. . . . " Despite his lack of fame and fortune, he added, if he had the chance he would "yet begin again with as small means as [he] did at first."[3]

It seems that Smith had no home to call his own during these years. While he may have rented rooms in St. Sepulchre's

Parish, one of the poorer districts of London, it seems that he spent much of his time visiting relatively wealthy friends. His last book was written at the country home of one such friend, Sir Humphrey Mildmay, where Smith lived as a guest in the fall of 1630.

From what he was writing in those days, it is obvious that John Smith was thinking of the end of his life. In one chapter in *Advertisements* he pays a great deal more attention to religious matters than he did in any of his other writings. This new focus on religion was also obvious in the fact that Smith dedicated the book to the Archbishop of Canterbury and the Archbishop of York. "My most Gracious Good Lords," he wrote in that dedication, "I desire to leave testimony to the world, how highly I honour as well the Miter as the Lance."[4] (A miter, or mitre, is a tall hat or headdress worn by bishops.)

There was good reason for Smith to focus on his own mortality. By June 1631, just a few months after he finished *Advertisements*, he was on his deathbed, probably in the house of Sir Samuel Saltonstall, a longtime friend. On June 21 of that year, Smith dictated his last will and testament.

In this will, he left to a friend the property in Lincolnshire that he had inherited from his father. A few other small bequests were made to other friends and to distant relations. Remarkably, given his history, his will included no weapons. Perhaps, in his financial need, John Smith had been forced to sell his arms, including the sword he wore when his portrait was painted. His bequests did, however, include several books. (Interestingly, the will of his contemporary, William Shakespeare, included weapons but no books.)

Sadly, we know but little about Smith's last days. We have no idea what disease killed him. It was not the plague, for London was free of that dreaded scourge in 1631. Whatever disease ended his life, it is to be hoped that he was not in pain—though if he was, he undoubtedly bore it well. Perhaps, if he was fortunate, he simply drifted off, perhaps dreaming as the darkness enveloped him. Perhaps he heard again the trumpets' blare and the clash of weapons he'd heard as a young man when he killed the three Turkish champions to earn his coat of arms and the right to call himself a gentleman. Maybe he smelled again the heady smells of Powhatan's Indian longhouse or the crisp, sweet air of a Chesapeake Bay winter. Perhaps, as John Smith lay dying, he imagined he was once again visited by Pocahontas, or felt again the rolling deck of a horizon-bound ship beneath his feet.

Of course we will never know. What we do know is that the man who had lived his entire life by his motto—"To Conquer is To Live"—met his final, unconquerable foe on June 21, 1631. At the time of his death, he was just fifty-one years of age.

In his will, Smith had put aside twenty pounds to pay for his funeral. Twenty pounds purchased a great deal in 1631. There was enough money to buy wine for the mourners, so glasses were undoubtedly raised in Smith's memory. His friends certainly must have gathered to laugh and perhaps cry together as they spoke of his adventures and exploits and mishaps. Then John Smith's remains were carried to a spot inside St. Sepulchre's Church in London, where he was laid to rest. In honor of his career as a soldier, a suit of armor—probably a funeral suit made for the occasion—would have been placed near his tomb. On the wall above his tomb a tablet was hung. On this tablet were the words:

> Here lies one conquer'd that hath conquered Kings,
> Subdu'd large Territories, and done things
> Which to the World impossible would seeme. . . .
>   But what availes his Conquest, now he lyes
> Inter'd in earth, a prey for Wormes and Flies?
> O may his soule in sweet Elizium sleepe,
> Untill the Keeper that all soules doth keepe,
> Returne to Judgement, and that after thence,
> With Angels he may have his recompense.[5]

In 1666, when the great fire of London lay waste to much of the city, the roof of St. Sepulchre's Church caught fire and collapsed. In the blaze, the tablet over Smith's grave was destroyed. The grave itself was consumed by the flames. While the lost tablet has been replaced with a brass replica, John Smith's bones were lost in the fire.

✦ Chronology ✦

1580 John Smith is born, probably in early January, in Lincolnshire, England.

1596 John's father dies. John leaves home to fight as a mercenary soldier in the Netherlands.

1599 John returns to England and learns horsemanship and the arts of combat.

1600 Smith departs for Eastern Europe. He joins the Christian forces battling the Turks, and earns a coat of arms for his valor in battle.

1602 Smith is captured in battle and sold into slavery.

1603 Smith escapes from his slave master and makes his way back to England, arriving in London in 1604.

1606 Smith and about 105 other settlers depart from England, bound for Virginia.

1607 On April 26, Smith and the other Virginia settlers arrive in the Chesapeake Bay.

Smith is captured by Indians and taken to the village of Powhatan, the Indian Emperor (early December).

Smith is saved by Pocahontas when her father, Powhatan, orders the Englishman's death (late December).

1608   Smith is injured by a stingray and almost dies (June).

John Smith is elected governor or "president" of the Jamestown Colony (September).

1609   A new charter is issued to the Virginia Company. John Smith is ordered removed from office (July).

The *Sea Venture*, with the colony's new leaders on board, is shipwrecked in the Bahamas Islands.

Smith is injured by an exploding bag of gunpowder (September).

John Smith departs from Virginia (October).

1610   Virginia, with Smith gone, goes through what has come to be known as the Starving Time.

1612   *A Map of Virginia* is published in London.

1614   John Smith maps the coastline of what is now Maine and Massachusetts. He names New England. He is named Admiral of New England by the Plymouth Company.

1616   Pocahontas comes to England. She and John Smith meet.

1617   Pocahontas dies in Gravesend.

1620   *New England Trials* is published in England.

1622   John Smith offers to lead a small army to Virginia to avenge the massacre of colonists.

1630   *The True Travels* is published in England.

1631   *Advertisements for the Unexperienced Planters of New England* is published.

John Smith dies (June).

❖ Source Notes ❖

CHAPTER ONE

1. John Smith, *The True Travels*. Included in *Works*, edited by Edward Arber (Westminster: Archibald Constable and Co., 1895), vol. II, p. 822.

2. *Ibid.*, p. 822.

3. *Ibid.*, p. 823.

4. Edward Arber (editor), *Works* (Westminster: Archibald Constable and Co., 1895), vol. I, p. xix.

5. John Smith, *op. cit.*, vol. II, p. 823.

6. *Ibid.*, p. 823.

7. *Ibid.*, p. 823.

8. *Ibid.*, p. 823.

CHAPTER TWO

1. John Smith, *The True Travels*. Included in *Works*, edited by Edward Arber (Westminster: Archibald Constable and Co., 1895), vol. II, p. 823.

2. *Ibid.*, p. 826.

3. *Ibid.*, p. 830.

4. *Ibid.*, p. 832.

5. *Ibid.*, p. 832.

6. *Ibid.*, p. 838.

7. *Ibid.*, p. 838.

8. *Ibid.*, p. 838.

9. *Ibid.*, p. 853.

10. *Ibid.*, p. 855.

11. *Ibid.*, p. 867.

CHAPTER THREE

1. Robert Gray, *A History of London* (London: Hutchinson & Co., 1978), p. 139.

2. Thomas Studley, et al., *The Proceedings of the English Colony in Virginia*. Included in *Works*, edited by Edward Arber (Westminster: Archibald Constable and Co., 1895), vol. I, p. 89.

3. Studley, p. 89.

4. John Smith, *New Englands Trials*. Included in *Works*, Vol. I, p. 242.

5. Alden Vaughan, *American Genesis* (New York: HarperCollins, 1975), pp. 20–21.

6. Philip Barbour, *The Three Worlds of Captain John Smith* (Boston: Houghton Mifflin Company, 1964), p. 417, note.

7. Vaughn, p. 21.

CHAPTER FOUR

1. Thomas Studley, et al., *The Proceedings of the English Colony in Virginia*. Included in *Works*, edited by Edward Arber (Westminster: Archibald Constable and Co., 1895), vol. I, p. 90.

2. John Morrill, editor, *Oxford Illustrated History of Tudor and Stuart Britain* (Oxford: Oxford University Press, 1996), p. 196.

3. Ivor N. Hume, *The Virginia Adventure* (Charlottesville: University Press of Virginia, 1994), p. 128.

4. George Percy, *Observations*. Included in *Works*, Vol. I, p. lvii.

5. John Smith, et al., *The Proceedings and Accidents of The English Colony in Virginia*. Included in *Works*, vol. II, p. 388.

6. George Percy, *op. cit.*, p. lvii.

7. *Ibid.*, p. lix.

8. John Smith, *The True Travels, Adventures, and Observations*. Included in *Works*, vol. II, p. 910.

9. George Percy, *op. cit.*, pp. lx–lxi.

10. John Smith, et al., *op. cit.*, p. 387.

CHAPTER FIVE

1. John Smith, *A Map of Virginia*. Included in *Works*, edited by Edward Arber (Westminster: Archibald Constable and Co., 1895), vol. I, p. 61.

2. *Ibid.*, vol. I, p. 48.

3. George Percy, *Observations*. Included in *Works*, vol. I, p. lxi.

4. *Ibid.*, vol. I, p. lxii.

5. Ivor Hume, *The Virginia Adventure* (Charlottesville: University Press of Virginia, 1994), p. 135.

CHAPTER SIX

1. John Smith, *Instructions by Way of Advice, etc.* Included in *Works*, edited by Edward Arber (Westminster: Archibald Constable and Co., 1895), vol. I, p. xxxiv.

2. *Ibid.*, vol. I, p. xxxv.

3. John Smith, *A True Relation*. Included in *Works*, vol. I, p. 6.

4. Thomas Studley, et al., *The Proceedings of the English Colony in Virginia*. Included in *Works*, vol. I, p. 90.

5. George Percy, *Observations Gathered out of a Discourse of the Plantation of the Southern Colonie in Virginia by the English, 1606*. Included in *Works*, vol. I, pp. lxviii–lxix.

6. Gabriel Archer, *A Relation of the Discovery, &c., 21 May – 22 June 1607*. Included in *Works*, vol. I, p. xli.

7. *Ibid.*, vol. I, p. l.

8. Thomas Studley, et al., *op. cit.* vol. I, p. 92.

9. *Ibid.*, vol. I, p. 93.

10. Quoted in Bradford Smith, *Captain John Smith, His Life and Legend* (New York: J.B. Lippincott, 1953), p. 101.

CHAPTER SEVEN

1. The London Company, *Instructions by Way of Advice, etc.* Included in *Works*, edited by Edward Arber (Westminster: Archibald Constable and Co., 1895), vol. I, p. xxxvii.

2. George Percy, *Observations*. Included in *Works*, vol. I, p. lxxi.

3. John Smith, *A True Relation*. Included in *Works*, vol. I, p. 8.

4. George Percy, *op. cit.*, vol. I, p. lxxii.

5. *Ibid.*, vol. I, pp. lxii–lxiii.

6. Edward Maria Wingfield, *A Discourse of Virginia*. Included in *Works*, vol. I, p. lxxvii.

7. John Smith, *op. cit.*, vol. I, p. 9.

8. John Smith, et al., *The Proceedings and Accidents of the English Colony in Virginia*. Included in *Works*, vol. II, p. 392.

9. John Smith, *op. cit.*, vol. I, p. 9.

10. *Ibid.*, vol. IX.

11. Thomas Studley, et al, *The Proceedings of the English Colony in Virginia*. Included in *Works*, vol. I, p. 96.

CHAPTER EIGHT

1. John Smith, *A True Relation*. Included in *Works*, edited by Edward Arber (Westminster: Archibald Constable and Co., 1895), p. 15.

2. *Ibid.*, p. 15.

3. John Smith, et al., *The Proceedings and Accidents of the English Colony in Virginia*. Included in *Works*, vol. II, p. 396.

4. *Ibid.*, p. 396.

5. *Ibid.*, p. 396.

6. *Ibid.*, p. 397.

7. *Ibid.*, p. 397.

8. *Ibid.*, p. 397.
9. *Ibid.*, pp. 399–400.
10. John Smith, *A True Relation*, vol. I, p. 38.
11. Francis Mossiker, *Pocahontas* (New York: Da Capo Press, 1996), p. 96.
12. Quoted in Mossiker, p. 96.

CHAPTER NINE
1. John Smith, et al., *The Proceedings and Accidents of the English Colony in Virginia*. Included in *Works*, edited by Edward Arber (Westminster: Archibald Constable and Co., 1895) vol. II, p. 400.
2. *Ibid.*, p. 401.
3. *Ibid.*, p. 401.
4. Edward Maria Wingfield, *A Discourse of Virginia*. Included in *Works*, vol. I, p. lxxxvi.
5. John Smith, *op. cit.*, p. 401.
6. *Ibid.*, p. 406.
7. *Ibid.*, p. 407.
8. *Ibid.*, p. 408.
9. John Smith, et al., *Advertisements: or, The Path-way to Experience to Erect a Plantation*. Included in *Works*, vol. II, p. 929.
10. John Smith, *op. cit.*, p. 414.
11. *Ibid.*, p. 420.

CHAPTER TEN
1. William Kelso, Nicholas Luccketti, and Beverly Straube, *James Towne Rediscovery IV* (Richmond: The Association for the Preservation of Virginia Antiquities, 1998), p. 25.
2. John Smith, et al., *The Proceedings and Accidents of the English Colony in Virginia*. Included in *Works*, edited by Edward Arber (Westminster: Archibald Constable and Co., 1895), vol. II, p. 436.
3. *Ibid.*, p. 436.

4. John Smith, *A Map of Virginia*. Included in *Works*, vol I, p. 46.

5. John Smith, et al., *op. cit.*, p. 437.

6. Quoted in Frances Mossiker, *Pocahontas* (New York: Da Capo Press, 1996), p. 38.

7. John Smith, *op. cit.*, p. 444.

8. *Ibid.*, p. 442.

9. *Ibid.*, p. 444.

10. *Ibid.*, p. 443.

11. *Ibid.*, p. 444.

12. *Ibid.*, p. 444.

13. Emerson Everett, *Captain John Smith* (New York: Twayne Publishers, 1971), p. 55.

14. *Ibid.*, p. 58.

15. John Smith, *op. cit.*, p. 144.

CHAPTER ELEVEN

1. John Smith, et al., *The Proceedings and Accidents of the English Colony in Virginia*. Included in *Works*, edited by Edward Arber (Westminster: Archibald Constable and Co., 1895), vol. II, p. 449.

2. *Ibid.*, p. 452.

3. Quoted in Bradford Smith, *Captain John Smith* (New York: J. B. Lippincott, 1953), p. 38.

4. John Smith, et al., *op. cit.*, p. 454.

5. *Ibid.*, p. 454.

6. *Ibid.*, p. 455.

7. *Ibid.*, p. 455.

8. *Ibid.*, p. 458.

9. *Ibid.*, p. 459.

10. *Ibid.*, pp. 462–63.

11. J. A. Leo Lemay, *The American Dream of Captain John Smith* (Charlottesville: University Press of Virginia, 1991), p. 116.

CHAPTER TWELVE

1. John Smith, et al., *The Proceedings and Accidents of the English Colony in Virginia*. Included in *Works*, edited by Edward Arber (Westminster: Archibald Constable and Co., 1895), vol. II, p. 449.

2. *Ibid.*, p. 471.

3. *Ibid.*, p. 472.

4. *Ibid.*, p. 476.

5. *Ibid.*, p. 477.

6. *Ibid.*, p. 480.

7. *Ibid.*, p. 484.

8. *Ibid.*

CHAPTER THIRTEEN

1. Quoted in Ivor N. Hume, *The Virginia Adventure*, (Charlottesville: University Press of Virginia, 1994), p. 258.

2. John Smith, et al., *The Proceedings and Accidents of the English Colony in Virginia*. Included in *Works*, edited by Edward Arber (Westminster: Archibald Constable and Co., 1895), vol. II, p. 499.

3. *Ibid.*, pp. 485–486.

4. Hume, *op. cit.*, p. 262.

5. John Smith, *The General History of New England*. Included in *Works*, vol. II, p. 697.

6. Quoted in Bradford Smith, *Captain John Smith* (New York: J. B. Lippincott, 1953), p. 192.

7. E. Keble Chatterton, *Captain John Smith* (New York: Harper & Brothers, 1927), p. 236.

8. Bradford Smith, *Captain John Smith* (Philadelphia: J. B. Lippincott, 1953), p. 288.

9. Quoted in Frances Mossiker, *Pocahontas* (New York: Da Capo Press, 1996), p. 274.

1. Quoted in Everett Emerson, *Captain John Smith* (New York: Twayne Publishers, 1971), p. 64.

2. Bradford Smith, *Captain John Smith* (New York: J. B. Lippincott, 1953), p. 290.

3. Philip Barbour, *The Three Worlds of Captain John Smith* (Boston: Houghton Mifflin, 1964), p. 390.

4. John Smith, *Advertisements for the Unexperienced Planters of New England*. Included in *Works*, edited by Edward Arber (Westminster: Archibald Constable and Co., 1895), vol. II, p. 920.

5. Bradford Smith, pp. 293–294.

✤ *Bibliography* ✤

JOHN SMITH'S WRITINGS

Smith, John. *Works.* 2 vols., edited by Edward Arber. Westminster: Archibald Constable and Co., 1895.

BIOGRAPHIES

Barbour, Philip. *The Three Worlds of Captain John Smith.* Boston: Houghton Mifflin, 1964.

Chatterton, E. Keble. *Captain John Smith.* New York: Harper & Brothers, 1927.

Emerson, Everett. *Captain John Smith.* New York: Twayne, 1971.

Smith, Bradford. *Captain John Smith.* New York: J. B. Lippincott, 1953.

Woods, Katherine Pearson. *The True Story of Captain John Smith.* New York: Doubleday, Page & Co., 1907.

OTHER SECONDARY SOURCES

Black, J. B. *The Reign of Elizabeth.* New York: Oxford University Press, 1994.

Gray, Robert. *A History of London.* London: Hutchinson & Co., 1978.

Hume, Ivor. *The Virginia Adventure.* Charlottesville: University Press of Virginia, 1994.

———. *Martin's Hundred*. New York: Knopf, 1982.

Lemay, J. A. Leo. *The American Dream of Captain John Smith*. Charlottesville: University Press of Virginia, 1991.

Middleton, Richard. *Colonial America, a History*. Oxford, UK: Blackwell, 1996.

Morgan, Ted. *Wilderness at Dawn*. New York: Simon & Schuster, 1993.

Mossiker, Frances. *Pocahontas*. New York: Da Capo Press, 1996.

Porter, Roy. *London, A Social History*. Cambridge, MA: Harvard University Press, 1995.

Quinn, Arthur. *A New World*. New York: Berkley Books, 1995.

Rowse, A. L. *The Elizabethans and America*. New York: Harper Colophon, 1959.

Vaughan, Alden. *American Genesis, Captain John Smith and the Founding of Virginia*. New York: HarperCollins, 1975.

Woodward, Grace Steele. *Pocahontas*. Norman: University of Oklahoma Press, 1969.

✦ Index ✦